Postcards from Nebraska

The Stories Behind the Stories
as seen on CBS News "Sunday Morning"
by
Roger Welsch
Essayist for CBS News "Sunday Morning"
and originator of "Postcards from Nebraska"

Photo Credits

Cover photo of Roger Welsch and Charles Kuralt: Linda Welsch

"Golden Harvest Time" (cover & page 13) courtesy Dept. of Economic Development, Nebraska Division of Tourism

"Native American Pow Wow" (cover & page 41) courtesy Dept. of Economic Development, Nebraska Division of Tourism

"Sandhill Cranes" (cover & page 115) courtesy Nebraska Game & Parks Commission

"Farmer's Market" (page 137) by Michael Forsberg, courtesy Dept. of Economic Development, Nebraska Division of Tourism

"Horseback Riding" (back cover) by Michael Forsberg, courtesy Dept. of Economic Development, Nebraska Division of Tourism

5 4 3 2
Printed in the United States of America

ISBN 0-934904-40-5

P.O. Box 5575
Lincoln, NE 68505

www.leebooksellers.com
e-mail: leebooks@radiks.net
1-888-655-0999

For Bud Lamoreaux, Iz Bleckman,
Dan Gianneschi, and Larry Gianneschi,
with gratitude . . .

Foreword

When Roger asked me to write this foreword for his book on CBS News Postcards from Nebraska, he triggered a kaleidoscope of images and memories that had been carefully filed away in my heart since the untimely death of our old friend Charles Kuralt on July 4, 1997.

My relationship with Charles flowed across a span of thirty years. The flow took us across "this America of ours"—Kuralt's words—and the stories he sent back to the CBS Evening News with Walter Cronkite read like conversations with old friends. He wrote about people who had never been seen before on television: brick makers, bridge builders, farmers, blacksmiths . . . Our rivers were the back roads and dirt lanes that crossed and recrossed the fast-flowing, multi-lane interstate highways that lace our country . . . paths that never tempted Charles to hop on and go with the flow. "Never know what's around the next bend" was a favorite Kuraltism. Our vessel was a Travco motor home, and its compass pointed us one day to Lincoln, Nebraska, where we pulled up to Roger Welsch's front porch so many summers ago.

Many people have been touched by Charles Kuralt, Roger and I among them. Thirty years ago I was given a gift. I got to work with Charles Kuralt and study television journalism with the master of the craft. In turn, Charles and I got to spend our time with the blacksmiths, boat builders, gandy dancers, moonshiners . . . even a musical saw player from the old vaudeville days. Al Zampa was an ironworker who helped build the Golden Gate Bridge. (For that story I climbed an iron ladder up the last twenty feet to the very top of the bridge, where the red aerolights shine at night!) Ben Green was an 80-year-old horse trader and storyteller from Cumby, Texas, who was also a graduate of the Edinburgh School of Veterinary Medicine. John Volker was a retired Supreme Court Justice of the State of Michigan who wrote books about the delicate art of fishing with the tiniest of flies tied to gossamer lines. Roger Welsch, a professor of English and anthropology at the University of Nebraska, when issued a ticket for the weeds in his front yard, ran for the office of county weed commissioner on a pro-weed ticket.

So many letters to America, so many wonderful stories, so many years have flown by. Roger and I have been touched by Charles Kuralt . . . perhaps even anointed, as if with a magic wand. A wave of it and I became his cameraman. Another pass and Roger was writing Postcards from Nebraska. Roger was already a published author when Charles suggested he try telling his stories in front of a camera. I think Charles knew that Roger had a natural talent for television. After we shot our second Postcard, I knew for certain that my camera and Roger were going to get along just fine.

As I look back over the past 13 years and almost 200 Postcards, I must thank Roger for the gift of working with another great story-teller. Photographing Postcards from Nebraska has been like watching Roger write this book, for every trip to Nebraska from Chicago I saw and heard new chapters spring from the landscape of the small towns and farms from one end of this state to the other. From behind my camera I watched Roger introduce his town of Dannebrog and its cast of memorable citizens to viewers of CBS "Sunday Morning."

It was no accident when Kuralt went off the road and onto "Sunday Morning" that he offered Roger the opportunity to write and host Postcards. I believe it was Charles' wish to insure that small-town America continue to have its stories told by a writer with empathy and talent.

Roger has done so . . . with much empathy and considerable talent. Charles was proud.

> — *Isadore Bleckman*
> *Cinematographer, CBS News*

Contents

Three men—a television cameraman, a sound technician, and a producer—were once walking along an ocean beach when one of them stumbled on something in the sand. He pulled it out and found it was a brass lantern—a magic lantern. He rubbed it and a huge genie suddenly appeared, announcing, "You each get one wish."

The cameraman said, "I've always wanted to be a rich man, lying on a nude beach in the south of France, surrounded by gorgeous women."

"You have it," the genie said, snapped his fingers, and the cameraman disappeared in a puff of smoke. "And what would you like?" he asked, turning to the soundman.

"All my life I've been attached to him by this audio cord," he said. "And I guess I'll stick with that. So, I'll take what he got."

The genie snapped his fingers again and the soundman disappeared in a puff of smoke too. "And you?" he said to the producer.

"I don't give a diddly damn what they want," the producer roared. "I want their butts back here, and I MEAN RIGHT NOW!"

The genie snapped his fingers . . .

An Introduction

I wish I could claim that my Postcards from Nebraska and my work with Charles Kuralt and CBS's "Sunday Morning" came about as a natural result of training, talent, and hard work on my part, or maybe my natural, rugged good looks. Or maybe by virtue of my pure intellectual power. But I can't. My decade of sending Postcards from Nebraska to America by way of CBS's "Sunday Morning" was dumb luck, pure and simple. Nothing but dumb luck, with more emphasis on "dumb" than I can comfortably admit.

It all started one day in 1972. My family was hot and tired after a long day's drive from Denver, where we had visited relatives, back to our Lincoln, Nebraska, home. The kids were growly and I wasn't much better. All that was about to change, but not for the better. I parked in the driveway behind the house and we emptied the luggage from the car. I stepped out the front door to assure myself that everything was okay at our modest, terminally suburban home. Everything looked fine.

Except for a pink sheet of paper taped to the storm door. It looked official, so I was already uneasy as I pulled it from the door's glass. I unfolded the paper and to my dismay read an official notice that I had six days to remove all "useless vegetation" from my lawn. Good God, my lawn had been condemned by the Lincoln city weed inspectors.

Or maybe that isn't where it all started. I suppose the pink notice was an inevitable culmination of where my life had been headed for years. Even though I was still relatively young (in my mid-30s), I was already uncomfortable with the suburban religion whose central belief is that bluegrass is sacred, and there shall be no other plants before it.

Scientifically and ecologically speaking, 100% bluegrass, putting-green lawns make no sense at all: anyone with even the most basic understanding of nature knows that a monoculture (one plant cultivated continuously and exclusively on the same ground over a long period of time) is a sure path to failure. You

1

can't grow corn and only corn on the same field for decade after decade without doing real damage to the soil, and eventually diminishing the crops harvested from that field. Or alfalfa, or tobacco, or tomatoes. And certainly, bluegrass.

Historically, the bluegrass lawn is too recent to have so completely taken over landscaping philosophies. Until fairly recently (the middle part of the twentieth century), a "lawn" was understood to be a kind of idyllic meadow, grasses mixed with wildflowers and herbs, filled with color, scents, and sounds—the precise opposite of today's "barefoot" lawns.

In keeping with that idea, the bluegrass lawn, with its dreary sameness, makes no aesthetic sense either. Religious zeal aside, the dandelion is a beautiful flower, after all. Okay, you think my lawn was weedy because I'm lazy, not for some high-flown ecological philosophy. Maybe there was some of that. Maybe both those factors were in play.

And more. For 10 years I'd developed an interest in wild plants as food and medicine, as a part of Plains pioneer history and as part of the living culture of Native American tribes, especially the Omaha. So I planted in my "lawn" jack-in-the-pulpit, calamus, cattails, catnip, Jerusalem artichokes, nut sedge, and dozens of other plants known to and used by nineteenth-century pioneers and Plains Indians but almost forgotten by us today. Forgotten, or called "useless vegetation" by dinky bureaucrats. Weeds. Yes, I had come to like weeds!

So, reflecting my interest in wild foods and medicines, my concern for the ecology, and my natural sloth, my lawn had become, I suppose, a little on the shaggy side. And it did stand out in the dreary monotony of the suburban street where we lived. And I'll admit it could have used a mowing. But "remove all useless vegetation"?! Fat chance.

I invited the Lincoln weed inspector to come out and show me exactly what he saw as "useless vegetation" in my, so to speak, lawn. The encounter went precisely as I expected. This poor boob reflected a bureaucratic mindlessness that wasn't even much fun to jerk around. "What's this white stuff over here?" he growled. He didn't know the name "lambs-quarters."

"Ate it for lunch. Guess it's not 'useless' then, huh?"

"Well, uh, what about this shaggy stuff there?"

"Sour dock. Having it for supper. Delicious. Better than lettuce. Sure as hell not 'useless.' Want a bite?"

We played that game for a while until he finally threw up his hands in frustration and played his ace. "In Lincoln, any plant over six inches tall is a weed," he snarled.

"And all weeds are useless, I suppose."

"You got it, buddy."

"Sweet corn? Hollyhocks? Day lilies? They're almost always more than six inches high."

"That's food and flowers, not weeds."

"These," I pointed to my weeds, "are food and flowers too."

"Weeds," he grumped, and left in an official cloud of dust.

I fought the city weed office for years, the situation never finding resolution. I found that the same Bluegrass-Ueber-Alles mentality dominated the Weed Board of Lancaster County, Nebraska, too. In a war against some truly troublesome weeds, like thistles and leafy spurge, blanket spraying was destroying entire landscapes. Ditches full of wild strawberries, elderberries, and chokecherries were obliterated by a deadly potion of 2,4-D and diesel fuel. While I could only frustrate and resist the dedicated officers of the city weed warriors, I discovered that members of the Lancaster Weed Control Authority were, aha! Elected!

So, I filled out my papers and launched my first (and only) political campaign. Despite the very real and serious dimensions of my concerns, my run for office was inescapably a light-hearted campaign. My bumper stickers read, "Welsch for Weed Board—Not Just Another Pretty Face." I was endorsed by Euell Gibbons, the first and most famous of the edible weed gurus.

And that's how I wound up on CBS's "Sunday Morning" with Charles Kuralt. No kidding.

Along Comes Kuralt

In 1972 (I've never known the precise date or organization or locale), but, as I understand it from Charles Kuralt, he was in Nebraska speaking to a group—maybe the Nebraska Press Association. During the banquet he asked the fellow sitting next to him if anything was going on in Nebraska that would make a good topic for one of his On the Road segments for the CBS Evening News.

"Well," Kuralt's dinner neighbor said, "there is this crackpot in Lincoln running for the Weed Board on a pro-weed ticket . . ."

In 1972 Kuralt's face and voice were already familiar to America, and he was a favorite in our household. As a folklorist, I was fascinated by his grasp of tradition, his access to tradition bearers, and his ability to say in a matter of minutes on television what academic folklorists still struggle for hours to explain in the classroom.

His telephone call hit our household like a bombshell: "Charles Kuralt is coming here, to our house!" And when the big On the Road van rolled up a couple weeks later, my lawn was suddenly trans-

3

formed from the neighborhood disgrace into a neighborhood celebrity. We whipped up a big weed salad, garnished it with edible flowers, filled Charles and his crew with wild grape wine, and generally got along famously.

Kuralt's visit had a lot of consequences, all of them good. First, I was elected to the Weed Board in a landslide. Over the course of my two terms in office, the mood of the board was changed by the election of other ecologists, and there was an emergence within the Board of naturalist inclinations on the part of veteran members so that the destructive policies of decades were reversed.

Secondly, Kuralt became my friend and my ideal as a writer and human being.

The third consequence of our meeting lay in the future. I had no hint of it on that summer afternoon in Lincoln. No, I take that back: A clue was there, but it was too subtle for me to recognize. Kuralt and I were leaning across a picket fence, ostensibly (for the camera) talking about weeds. Actually, I was taking advantage of the quiet moment in our frantic day of shooting to pass along a message any number of friends had asked me to give him. "You know, Charles," I said, "everyone has told me to tell you they envy you because you have the greatest job in the world—traveling around, meeting people, talking about interesting things, seeing fascinating places."

Without hesitation he responded, "No, Roger. You have the best job in the world. As a folklorist in Nebraska, you meet remarkable people, you talk about interesting things, you see fascinating places. And you don't have to travel around. Tomorrow I'll be in Wyoming or Nevada or who knows where, wishing I'd had more time to talk with you. But my job doesn't let me do that. You? You'll still be here, talking to the pioneers and Indians about their plants. When you get interested in something, you have the luxury of the time to explore that idea, to get to know the people and geography it reflects. No, my friend, I don't have the best job in the world. You have the best job in the world."

It wasn't just something he said by way of a courtesy to his host. Many times he expressed the same idea to me. He felt that his first marriage was destroyed by his travels. I once kidded him about still being in love with his first wife—and I could tell from the look on his face that it was no laughing matter. Perhaps the most poignant indication of how this wanderlust in his life had been both a boon and curse was an inscription he wrote in a copy of his book, *Charles Kuralt: A Life on the Road:* "For Roger—who had sense enough to stay home beside the Loup. With affection and admiration of his old friend, Charles Kuralt."

Over the next 15 years Charles and his van and his crew—Larry Gianneschi, soundman, and Izzy Bleckman, cinematographer—visited us every year or so. I kept a file of "On the Road" ideas for Charles and when he came visiting, we'd sit down and thumb through it. He would ask me what I was up to, I'd tell him, and more often than not, he would say, "Hell, Rog, that's an On the Road story right there! Do you have some time tomorrow to do a little shooting?" And in an easy afternoon we would crank out a piece, and then spend an evening eating, drinking, and laughing over Peking Duck at Lincoln's Imperial Palace restaurant.

In 1988 I left the University of Nebraska, where I had an appointment as a professor of English and anthropology, to move out to a small tree farm I had owned and built up for a dozen years. My daughter Antonia was about to start school, and I wanted her to grow up in small-town America; I wanted to spend whatever I had left of my life in Dannebrog (population 324) with my friends, and I wanted to be closer to the folklore and tradition I studied and wrote about. I hoped to make a living writing and speaking.

But it didn't work out quite that way. After six months I had to tell my wife Linda that we weren't making it financially, "living on my good looks," but that I couldn't bring myself to going back to teaching in the city. Linda said she would do whatever she could to keep us going financially—get a job in town maybe—and with that new resolve, we decided to stick it out on the Dannebrog farm.

The next month Charles Kuralt was passing through Nebraska, near where I was giving a banquet speech for a small-town chamber of commerce banquet. He came to the banquet hall—causing quite a stir, as you can imagine, and while Iz Bleckman and Larry Gianneschi drove the legendary On the Road van toward Lincoln, Charles rode with me in my car. During that ride through a rainy Nebraska night he asked me how I would feel about working for money instead of for free for a change. I told him it sure sounded like a good idea. A super idea, in fact!

Kuralt's idea was to add to his show "Sunday Morning," then only seven years old, a series of "postcards," sent by various friends of his from around America. "Sunday Morning" was a mirror image of Kuralt's mind, a collection of his friends and interests, presented in his comfortable, easy way. While he was pleased that the show was successful in bringing ballet, theater, book reviews, history, nature, science, and jazz to backwater places like Dannebrog, where such ideas tend to get rare attention, he knew that things go on in small towns that deserve attention too, and are worth bringing to the folks

5

in the big cities. Tim Sample would send a Postcard from Maine, Molly Ivins from Texas—me from Nebraska.

You can bet I didn't sleep much that night. It was one thing to be in front of the camera with Charles, but by myself? That was a different matter altogether. But it was also an opportunity I couldn't pass up. For one thing, the money involved certainly wasn't enough to live on, but it could make the difference for us surviving on the farm. Secondly, I feel strongly about the things I work with: rural humor, pioneer ingenuity, Native American culture. And with evangelistic fervor, I've always felt driven to tell others about them. What a chance this would be to do precisely that!

For the first four Postcards from Nebraska, Charles came to Dannebrog with his old crew, by now my old friends too—Izzy and Larry. I was a little nervous about the prospect, but I presumed that I'd settle down all right because, after all, Kuralt and I had worked together in front of the camera a dozen times before. But the work was tougher than I expected, looking at the camera and seeing Charles Kuralt there behind it, the master writer and television reporter watching me in my first, clumsy efforts.

I stuttered, stammered, stumbled. Finally, Charles pushed his glasses down his nose, as he used to do, and said, "Roger, just try to forget there are five million households on the other side of the camera." The look on my face completely broke up Izzy and Larry, and eventually me. It was obvious that Charles did forget all those people are out there. To him, they were just friends. That light-hearted moment did the job.

I still feel an enormous obligation (mostly to America, my rural neighbors, and Charles Kuralt) when I do my Postcards from Nebraska, but now I can indeed forget that there are five million households on the other side of that camera and talk pretty much about what I would talk about if I were in Eric's Tavern exchanging ideas with you over a cold beer.

Finding the Look

By way of experimentation in that first set of four stories, for one piece (I think it was about bullet holes in highway signs) I wore slacks and an open-neck sport shirt. For the Postcard about New York (one of the very few pieces we shot that died before being broadcast) I wore a sport coat, tie, and slacks. For another (on the post office, I believe) it was jeans and a flannel shirt. Since the fourth story was about the protocol of wearing overalls, naturally I wore overalls.

A couple weeks after Charles and his crew left Nebraska, he called and said that the editing was going well. "But I can tell you one thing," he said. "The only piece you really look comfortable in is the one about overalls."

"That's because I was comfortable," I said. "Most of my friends wear overalls. I wear overalls every day around here. Wearing a coat, even without a tie, is just not my style."

"Well, then that's it," he said. "Wear overalls."

And that's the way it was for the next 10 years. For the next set of Postcards, E. S. "Bud" Lamoreaux, senior producer of "Sunday Morning," came to Nebraska with Larry and Izzy, and he said the same thing. Except maybe not as diplomatically. "With a potato face like yours," he said, "the overalls will be a trademark. They'll never recognize your face, or your voice, or this dreary landscape, but they will recognize the overalls."

Bud and Charles were right. Occasionally a Nebraskan complains that my overalls reflect badly on our state, giving folks around America the idea that Nebraska is a, well, rural state. In response I explain that Nebraska *is* a rural state, and I cannot for the life of me imagine why anyone would be embarrassed by that. That usually quiets the complainer (who is nearly always from Omaha, incidentally).

But when I stroll through an airport in my overalls (the most comfortable flying clothes you can imagine), Charles and Bud's wisdom becomes evident: "Hey, Kansas! Love your pieces on . . . uh . . . 20/20." They get the state wrong, and the show, and the network, but they recognize the overalls. (Sure glad that first piece I did for "Sunday Morning" wasn't about men who wear pantyhose!)

So, for many years Bud, Izzy, and Larry came to Nebraska every other month to spend a week shooting another four Postcards. When Larry retired in 1992, his son Dan Gianneschi took over his father's earphones, keeping our Postcards from Nebraska family together. By now Dan, Iz, Larry, and Bud have become honorary citizens of Nebraska and Dannebrog, and of our family. At the time of this writing, late 1999, we have written, shot, and aired nearly 180 Postcards and Dannebrog, Nebraska, is probably the best documented rural town in all of network television history next to Mayberry.

As it turned out, our format has been steady and consistent over the years: a five- to six-minute essay, usually with me doing an on-camera introduction and close, and maybe a stand-up, with usually an interview somewhere in the middle. I have indeed focused on small-town and rural life, but my main intent has been to say something with a meaning beyond interesting pictures. I believe there is profound meaning to almost every facet of life, and I have wanted to encourage others to think about it just as I have.

We wound up doing two Postcards a month, sometimes even three, and then when Tim Sample joined the cast of "Sunday Morning," I was cut back to one. I really didn't mind that. I was troubled by the unfortunate drift of purpose in the Postcards—for that matter, in "Sunday Morning" in general—as the focus on meaning grew ever more shallow and the appeal to pretty pictures grew ever stronger. I'll tell you all about those problems a little later. It doesn't matter. My hope has only been to show and tell the stories I want to pass along, and Charles Kuralt gave me that opportunity.

Now I did have the almost perfect job. I was on one of the most prestigious, certainly one of the most beloved news shows on television, and yet I didn't have to be a journalist, or reporter. I consider myself an essayist. Kuralt warned me at the time that television is no place for writers, and he certainly was right, but being an essayist is a great place for an opinionated campaigner, and being on "Sunday Morning" is a great place for a student of culture, high and low.

For a while I bristled when Republicans and other fools unloaded blame for everything from Reagan's obscene budgets to bad weather on "the media," in part, I suppose, because I thought they were talking about me. But it soon became clear that while I was known to some as a television personality, I was not understood to be a part of the insidious and subversive "media." Maybe no one is. I get the feeling sometimes that "the media" is simply a nonexistent boogeyman.

A Celebration of the Typical

Anyway, Kuralt's master plan was realized, so I enjoyed a marvelous Postcard monopoly for six years. As time passed it became clear to me that my task was not at all to send a Postcard from Nebraska. My contributions therefore became less and less about Dannebrog or Nebraska or even the Plains, and increasingly dealt with life in small-town and rural America. I've come to appreciate most of all those letters from viewers that say, "What's with the fat guy in overalls from Nebraska? We have fat guys in overalls in Indiana too!"

That, of course, is precisely the point. Kuralt has come to refer to Postcards from Nebraska as "a celebration of the typical," and that's fine with me. Eugenia Zuckerman deals with the extraordinary in music, John Leonard with the remarkable in literature and drama, Billy Taylor with giants of jazz. I like to think there should be a few minutes a month to celebrate the typical, since that's what most of us, most Americans for that matter, are: typical, and I think we're a pretty interesting lot.

Putting Postcards from Nebraska together hasn't always been easy. In my normal life I sit here in my office, looking out over the Highway 58 bridge over the lazy Middle Loup River. I spend an hour or two an afternoon out in my machine shop working on old tractors. I toss a Frisbee for the dogs now and then. Afternoons before dinner, I go up to the town tavern for a beer or two with my cronies.

And then out of nowhere come Bud, Izzy, and Dan, "The Breeze Brothers," as we have come to know them, for their "breezing in and breezing out," or "The Scud Bubbas," in honor of the erratic, unpredictable, more-annoying-than-dangerous unguided missiles of Gulf War fame. Then they leave me to clean up the messes they leave behind. Izzy and Dan are from Chicago; Bud is from New York. They operate with an urban spirit of frenzy and fury. Sometimes I find myself listening to three sets of instructions at once. Then they "breeze off," or explode harmlessly in the Nebraska desert, and I find myself exhausted and shattered, my blood pressure off the top of the scale, my nerves shaky.

Over the years however I've come to understand that for all the fuss and fury, Izzy, Dan, and Bud are my friends and their first concern is to make me look good, to bring my stories to life. I have often wondered why these guys work so hard when they enjoy so little appreciation from CBS News (their names don't even appear on the "Sunday Morning" credits). But now I think it's because they are my friends and want to do their best for me and because they are dedicated professionals, intent on doing their best, appreciation or not. After all, they did the same for Charles Kuralt himself!

In fact, after one year of working with Bud, I wrote a desperate letter to Charles: "Bud Lamoreaux is impossible. I don't see how I can continue to work with him. I am seriously thinking of asking for release from my contract so I can resign from the show." Charles and I were both going to be in Washington, D.C., for the National Endowment for the Arts National Heritage Awards, and I wondered if we might not meet and talk this matter over.

Charles agreed and so we met on a pleasant September morning somewhere near the campus of George Washington University. For an hour I explained how Bud changed my scripts without so much as a word of apology, or explanation. Without apparent reason or pattern he rejected some scripts, and completely changed others without consulting with me. He mutilated my words, and worse yet my ideas. He missed my point. He didn't seem to understand my point of view, my intent, my argument, my poetry.

As lunchtime approached, Charles and I went into a small restaurant for a salad and a sandwich and I continued my complaint. After we ate, I detailed still more grievances against Bud over a bottle of wine. "He's not just difficult, Charles—he's impossible."

When I finally ran out of material and breath, Charles sat quietly considering my presentation for a while, looked me straight in the eye, and said, "Do you want my honest opinion here, Roger?"

"Of course," I said. "That is precisely what I want."

Charles looked me in the eye. He sipped his glass of wine. And he said, "Shut up and do what Bud says."

After the shock wore off, I said, "Okay. That's all I really needed—someone to explain things to me!"

And then Charles did explain. He told me that Bud is brash because he's a producer, abrasive because he's a New Yorker, hard-nosed because he's a professional, intent because he cares about CBS and "Sunday Morning," insistent because he cares about me. "He likes you," Charles said, "and all he is trying do is make you look as good as he can as quickly and efficiently as he can."

I have come to understand that and believe it. Izzy, Dan (and earlier Larry), and I have had to shoot a few pieces on our own, and there's been little doubt how much we missed Bud's direction. And I can't even remember how many times we've sent Bud back to New York with a few cassettes of tape and a lot of question of whether we actually had anything on them worth airing. Bud has never failed to rescue us, producing truly splendid silk purses out of thoroughly ragged sows' ears.

Millions of Friends

So, this set of print essays about television essays is dedicated to my second family, Larry Gianneschi, Dan Gianneschi, Isadore Bleckman, and E. S. "Bud" Lamoreaux—the Breeze Brothers, the Scud Bubbas, The Boys. Of all the gifts Charles Kuralt brought to my life with his kindness those 25 years I knew him, nothing comes close to the friends he gave me in these guys.

And you. Along with the wonderful gift of having a couple hundred chances to say what I want to say to an audience of six or eight million people, Kuralt gave me six or eight million new friends. Over the past 10 years I've gotten a dozen or two letters a week from viewers—a few gripers, a lot of friendly hellos, thank-yous, and story ideas. I've tried to answer all of them except for the truly rude ones, which I have thrown away without reading further the moment I detected the nature of the insults.

I have been waved at, talked with, encouraged at airports, hotels, and little produce stands near the beach at Akumal, Mexico, a thousand times. And I have loved every one of those times. Now, I want to make it clear that that's not so much a tribute to my work as it is to the kind of people who watch "Sunday Morning." Although that seems like too modest a word for what "Sunday Morning" viewers do—"watch." "Sunday Morning" viewers are more like a congregation than an audience. Almost every time a "Sunday Morning" fan says, "I watch that show religiously . . . ," they add, ". . . and I mean that: religiously!"

Yes, there have been times when the modest fame "Sunday Morning" has brought me wasn't all that welcome. People have driven into our farmyard at all hours, day and night, every day of the week and year, ignoring our pleas for privacy, the signs warning them about the dogs, and the snarling of the dogs themselves. Uninvited visitors have walked past all the signs and the dogs and an angry wife to knock at our door, wanting an hour or so to sit on the back porch, drink lemonade, and chat. I guess I have made writing look like too easy a job—actually no job at all.

I think the last straw was the day 12 separate carloads of tourists rolled into our place, each full of wonderful, pleasant people, each wanting only a half hour of so of my time, each thereby destroying whatever chance I had that day to get any work done, or to find any comfort.

I have tried to make it clear that all I ask by way of privacy is my little patch of 60 acres on the Middle Loup River; within the entire rest of the world I consider myself fair game. I think the worst time was the occasion when I was standing at a urinal in O'Hare Airport and the fellow next to me recognized me and reached across the divider between stalls to shake hands with me. I begged off, noting that my right hand was, er, kind of busy.

Now, believe me, I'm not complaining. It's flattering knowing that I have made myself such a member of the nation's households that people feel perfectly comfortable in driving in and making themselves at home here. I have had to send them firmly away, but I have inevitably felt renewed gratitude to Charles Kuralt for giving me that chance to be an American friend.

So there it is: a friend of television stars like Charles Kuralt and Bill Geist, a friend of wonderful craftsmen like Iz Bleckman, Bud Lamoreaux, and the Gianneschis, and a friend of millions and millions of Americans who have the good sense and good taste to watch a show of the quality of "Sunday Morning."

All that from not mowing my lawn. There's got to be a moral there somewhere.

In addition to Bud, Dan, Larry, and Iz, I am grateful to my wife Linda for all she has done to get me through my weeks with Bud,

Dan, Larry, and Iz, and to recover afterward. Thanks too to good friends like Dick Day, Peg Briggs, John Carter, Mary Ethel Emanuel, and all the others who have helped me with ideas, background material, support, good cheer, and humor, in Dannebrog and every other Nebraska community where we have shown up with a thousand questions and requests.

*Your Favorite
Postcards from
Nebraska*

The Smokehouse

Of the 150 or so Postcards I have sent over nearly a decade with "Sunday Morning", it was one of the most simple that excited the most response, a short report on something I do every year, CBS or not—smoking hams and bacon in my smokehouse.

Bud, Iz, Larry, and I had our doubts about the script: one of Charles Kuralt's personal rules is referred to at CBS as the Tricycle Theory: "If you are doing a story about a fat guy who rides a tricycle, *you* don't get on the tricycle." It's the sort of idea you never really think a lot about until you hear it put together in words and start watching television with it in mind. As usual, Kuralt was absolutely right. Riding that tricycle makes you look stupid and kills whatever story the guy with the tricycle had to tell in the first place.

Watch any television show, "Sunday Morning" included, and when you see a reporter, reviewer, or essayist, "ride the tricycle" you will see someone making a damn fool of himself. And his viewers.

For a good part of the previous 20 years I had smoked meat, rubbing hams and bacon slabs with a mixture of curing salt, saltpeter, brown sugar, molasses, and just a dash of Tabasco sauce, waiting until the deepest, bitterest cold of winter to insure that the meat would take on its smoky color and taste, but not cook (or even stay warm) in the cramped quarters of my six-by-eight smokehouse.

I pack the hams and bacon in plastic garbage cans and let them soak in the cure for a week or so in my garage or shop. Every couple days I fish them out, rub them again, and repack them. Then I pull them from the briny syrup, rinse them off (cold business in a Nebraska winter!) put them on a sled made out of an old car hood, and slide them behind a tractor down to the smoker.

I pull heavy cord or wire through the shank end of the hams and hang them from stout wires on poles spanning the top plates of the smokehouse's low walls. (Which reminds me, I promised myself last winter I would put some bracing wires on those poles. I didn't like the way they bent and groaned under the weight of the 30 hams I hung on them this past winter.)

I like a fire of green or slightly wet apple wood and corncobs. Nothing gives a sweeter smoke than cobs. Three or four times a day, starting at dawn and ending just before we go to bed, I walk or drive the tractor through the snow down to the smokehouse, stoke the fire, check to make sure the smoke-house door is secure against coyotes and raccoons, and generally enjoy the sight of those beautiful, brown hams hanging quietly from their racks, growing browner by the hour.

There's no question about it, home-cured and smoked ham is better than the pinkish, water-logged stuff you buy in a modern grocery store, but most of all I like the ritual of celebrating the winter solstice in my quiet, hidden "temple" with this ancient ceremony of incense and sacrifice.

After a few days of this I pull all the meat from the cold smokehouse, and then comes the real fun. Every year I put between 30 and 40 hams through this process. Most of them are shoulder, or "picnic," hams, but still, that's a lot of meat, way too much for our little household freezer. So, since we give away all but a few of them for Christmas presents anyway, Christmas or not, I just load up my old Ford pickup with hams and ricochet across the Howard County, Nebraska, landscape delivering early Christmas presents pretty much most of the day. I am proud of my hams and I know they are special presents. A home-cured, home-smoked ham is always special, so I am about as welcome as a visitor can be, next to Santa.

Hamming it Up

Bud Lamoreaux, senior producer of "Sunday Morning," and I worried about doing a story about something I just do as a normal part of my annual activities. Was I doing a story about myself? Is that riding the tricycle? Well, we decided, not in this case, since I really am the guy who rides the tricycle! And as it turned out, the star of the piece was not me, but the smokehouse, those beautiful hams, and some spectacular weather.

With most Postcards we can start just about any time, but the hams have their own schedule. I started curing the hams 10 days before the crew came into Nebraska, and just had to hope the weather would be cold enough for smoking. A couple days before they arrived to shoot the story, we had a beautiful, fluffy snow and the farm looked like something out of a hokey Jimmy Stewart movie. I went down to the smokehouse to make sure everything was ready for the hams, walking a roundabout path so when the time came for the shoot we could get shots of my old International 300 tractor rolling through the untracked, sparkling, pristine snow. Everything was beautiful and ready.

I can't even remember how many times we've been frustrated in shooting a story, annoyed, or even stopped by Nebraska's fickle weather, but this time everything was perfect. It was cold enough that my breath showed, but not so cold that the camera froze up; the snow crunched, but the tractor started; I was cold, but not miserable; the sun was shining so that the snow was sparkling, but it wasn't so intense that the snow was melting.

Everything went well with the shoot, the hams accumulating pair by pair on the poles in the smokehouse rafters . . . until Bud decided he needed a "revealing shot." He thought it would really set things off if Izzy went way into the back of the pitch-black smokehouse, back behind and under the dripping hams, and got a shot of me, with the light behind me, opening the door and coming in with a couple hams in my hands. I was to hang them on a roof pole and start up my smoking fire, then eye the groaning poles appreciatively through the growing cloud of smoke, turn, and exit the smokehouse, leaving the hams—and Izzy—behind me in the dark.

Izzy, ever the fearless cinematographer, groaned audibly. We looked at him with amazement. He'd never been afraid of snakes, spiders, the dark, roaring fires, crashing machinery, groaning bridges, anything before, and now he was reluctant to spend a few minutes in the dark of my innocuous smokehouse?

"I didn't mind shooting this story with you, Rog," he said apologetically, "and I didn't even mind when I had to stick my camera into that brine barrel full of pork. It was all right when I had to run along behind the tractor, in the snow, to get the shot of you going through the trees with the rear ends of 15 or 20 pigs, and I didn't even complain when Bud made me shoot you carrying all that bacon over your shoulder into the smoker. But I can't help but wonder what the world is coming to when a poor Jewish boy like me has to get back there under all those dripping hams in a cold, pitch-black shed . . . ON HANUKKAH MORNING!"

Whoops.

Izzy did get the shot for Bud, and restrained himself to just a few comments that evening when we taped the closing shot of my circle of friends gathered around our table eating one of those big, lovely hams. (Linda had roast beef for Izzy.)

Kuralt later told me that he had been at a very elegant and high-level dinner party where the topic of the Nebraska Postcards arose.

Larry Tisch, then CEO of CBS, announced that his favorite Postcard was the one about the smokehouse and the hams, and Charles laughed, "You know you're doing all right, Rog, when you do a story about pork and even your Jewish friends like it."

The bulk of the mail I received about that Postcard was from folks asking for my recipe for hams. My mother asked my grandmother once for her recipe for runzas, a traditional meat pie in my father's family. Grandma was baffled by the notion. A recipe? Why, it's a matter of a "podja" (a handful) of this and a "podja" of that, and then you knead it all until it feels right, and heat the oven until it's ready, and cook it until it's done.

How much brown sugar or molasses do I use in my ham cure? Well, as much as we have on hand and I can find on the shelves of the local grocery store.

How long do I leave the hams in the brine? Until it's cold enough to build a fire in the smokehouse.

How long do the hams hang in the smoke? Until I run out of patience and have a nice day to drive the back roads of Howard County, passing out hams to all our friends.

Maybe the whole process is just too complicated to write down—at least emotionally.

Trains

One of the first Postcards I sent to "Sunday Morning" was a baldfaced effort to get myself a ride in a train engine. Trains are one of the greatest mysteries of the human psyche, in my opinion. Thoreau, the romantic lover of nature and the earth untrammeled by human industry, used to walk to a railroad track near Walden Pond to watch the steam engines roar by. As a folklorist, I have always been attracted to alternate technology, the quiet mechanisms of tradition that the automobile, airplane, and railroads have wreaked such havoc upon. And yet I don't know of any ecologists, nature nuts, primitives, or recluses who hate trains. There's just something about trains.

I know there are people who get furious when they have to stop at a crossing and wait a couple minutes for a train to pass by before them. Some risk their lives to avoid the agony of the experience. Not me. I never get tired of watching the cars flash by—empty ones, dirty ones, old ones, new ones—makes no difference to me.

I resent the sound of traffic in the middle of the night on the highway that runs by our farm. But like the song of the coyote, the dull thud of coal trains running on a track about 10 miles south (yes, we can hear them that far away) is like music. I wonder about the gigantic quantities of Wyoming that are passing through Nebraska on a relentless schedule without there being, visibly, any less of Wyoming. I wonder about the weight that goes through Nebraska in a day, in a year, and try to calculate what happens to the earth when that much of its mantel is transplanted 1000 miles or so in advance of its rotation.

In the Postcard from Nebraska essay I wrote about coal trains, was a tongue-in-cheek suggestion about all those empty coal cars coming back through Nebraska after their black loads had been dumped at power stations in New Jersey, Illinois, and Tennessee. Why, I asked, couldn't they come back with all that garbage the cities were having trouble getting rid of? Or all the snow that clogs eastern cities in the winter? The snow could be dumped on the naked plains of Wyoming and from there it could run back downhill through Nebraska, where we need the water for irrigating crops and generating even more power. The garbage could be tucked into the holes from which, I presume, gigantic machines are grinding millions of tons of coal. I'd cover it with the rock overburden that is probably just cast aside in the mining operation, and the huge garbage pie could start all over again on the million-year process of making more coal.

Well, that may have been my story, but what I really intended to do was finagle a way to get into the locomotive of a rolling train. It wouldn't make any sense at all to do an essay on trains and not have at least one of my on-cameras on the train, right? No doubt about it, I was going to get my train ride, even though my plan was a trifle devious.

And a trifle too much like those legendary best-laid plans that often go astray.

The crew taped trains rolling by various sites near the farm and then we drove our equipment van 30 miles up the track to Ravenna, Nebraska, where we could catch a coal train temporarily at rest. And get on board. I could hardly wait.

We got to Ravenna, made our contacts, got the shots we needed in the rail yard, and got ready to travel with the train back to Grand Island. "Rog," Bud said—and I knew from the tone of his voice exactly what was coming—"We'll shoot the footage in the engine on the ride back to Grand Island. Here are the keys to the van. We'll meet you at the Highway 281 overpass in Grand Island."

My disappointment must have been visible, but Bud is not the sort of guy who is moved by sympathy, especially for me. He not only laughed at me on that occasion, he laughed at me almost every time we saw a train anywhere, anytime, over the next four years of taping. You need to know Bud and his, uh, special talent for this sort of thing.

To give you some idea of how it goes, the crew and I were once enjoying supper at Grand Island's Yen Ching restaurant, one of our favorite dining spots, especially when it was the last night of a shoot, when everything was tucked away on tape and the worst part of the work was over. Izzy and I were admiring one of the waitresses, a stunningly beautiful, young Asian woman. We were absolutely dumbstruck by her beauty. Iz said, "That does it. I'm going to propose to her when she comes back to take our orders. I'm just going to sign the house and all my accounts over to her and ask her only that in return I get to live in the house with her and see her loveliness every day for the rest of my life. Yep, that's it. I'm going to propose."

Now, I'm a married man, so my fantasies were naturally a trifle more restrained than Izzy's, and a lot less likely, but I suggested some equally stupid, sexist, depraved and lustful course of action, and we watched the young woman as she moved around the room. Eventually she came back to our table, but before Iz could propose (or, as is more likely, order fried wontons), Bud struck up a conversation with her. We were all a little taken aback. That's not like Bud. He orders what he wants to eat or drink and that's pretty much it. A flirt, he's not.

"Did you come to this country recently?" he asked her, and she said she'd been here about a year. "And where are you from?" he asked, and they talked about Asian geography a little. Still no clue why Bud had engaged this conversation, no suggestion where it was going.

"Do you have a family?" he asked, and then it began to dawn on us. For five minutes Bud talked with the young lady about her husband and children and happy family and on and on, utterly demolishing our lascivious, sexist babbling with genteel thoughts of family, motherhood, pretty babies, and loving husbands. When she left our table, Bud simply looked across at us with a leer of victory, and laughed and laughed and laughed and laughed.

That's the kind of cruel sense of humor he has, and that's pretty much the way he handled the matter of my aborted fantasy of a ride on a real train.

UP Engine #3985

I made it clear, therefore, when I sent Bud my script for yet another train story—the maiden voyage of the mighty Union Pacific steamer #3985 across Nebraska—that there was no way in hell I would miss this ride, that violence was not at all out of the question. He did not rise to my threats.

We drove 150 miles west of Dannebrog to North Platte, Nebraska, to meet the great beast of an engine, and the moment we saw the huge restored steam engine, Bud knew this was not going to be a joking matter.

That curious romantic love affair all men have with steam engines struck me like Marilyn Monroe used to strike adolescent boys. At the time we shot our story on engine #3985, I was not a mechanic (I have since become one, sort of). In fact, I held an intense dislike for anything mechanical. I still feel that way about automobiles. But this thing, UP Engine #3985, is not machinery.

It is a living, breathing being as unlikely and as alive as a sperm whale, no less awesome, no less inspiring. I just stood there and stared, my mouth hanging agape. The engine was standing in the North Platte rail yard but it wasn't at rest. Oil glistened from its flanks like sweat. Steam breathed in pulses from valves and vents. Men swarmed over her, lubricating, watering, adjusting, tightening. Others, like me, just stood and stared.

Engine #3985 is as long as a football field. It is articulated—that is, the frame hinges in the middle so it can make the rail curves built for other, more mortal engines. (The huge boiler is not hinged, just the frame under it, so when it rounds curves, the wheels follow the rails while the huge superstructure of the engine continues to point where inertia would take it rather than where the man at the throttle wants it to go.) It is the largest rolling steam engine operating in the world today.

The Union Pacific railroad operates the engine, but (I love this part of the story) did not restore it. UP employees restored the engine with their own time and money, which should silence any who doubt my theory about the magical attraction steam engines and railroads have for all men, and maybe some women, I don't know. These people who worked so hard at their day-to-day work and for whom time away from work (trains, train business, engines, rails, and ties) is so precious, spent some of that valuable time caressing this gorgeous old engine back into running condition.

And Bud knew that there was no way he'd be able to vex my dreams about riding in that engine, that I would walk right over the top of him, no matter what he thought or decided.

I spent hours standing by the engine, watching it, feeling it, listening to it, smelling, and watching others who were watching, feeling, listening to, and smelling it. I cannot describe the experience without sounding like a goofy romantic because that's exactly what I was. It's what I am.

As night fell, all the subtleties continued, only enhanced by artificial lights. It turned out that the engine never sleeps. Its fires continue, subdued but still hot. The thing is alive. It is not machinery. I finally went to bed that night, satisfied that nothing is as beautiful, ever has been as beautiful as that engine standing like a football-field-long black Labrador dog.

The next day changed my mind. There is something more beautiful than the UP Engine #3985 at rest—the UP Engine #3985 in full roar. (Sitting here at my word processor, just remembering that day, my skin crawls with goose bumps.) Knowing he had no choice whatsoever, Bud told me to get into the engine. We would shoot at least one on-camera in the cab, and probably some b-roll (background footage), and besides, we needed the van to get rolling shots of the train in action, and if I were in the van I would only crowd the camera and soundman.

"And besides," he laughed, "I get the feeling you'd kill anyone who got between you and that engine."

If the potential power of that engine bowled me over, the energy realized almost destroyed me. I simply could not believe it. The fury of the sound, heat, smoke, vibration, and wind in the cab of that train going 65 miles an hour was like nothing I have ever experienced before.

And, just like in the North Platte rail yard, a good part of the experience was seeing the faces of the people lining the track as we thundered by: little kids with eyes as big as dinner plates, old men almost weeping with the force of their memories. I have never seen so many unblinking eyes and open mouths. At every crossing there were clumps of people, some with cameras, some with tape recorders, some waving. Lots with babies; parents or grandparents holding them aloft to see this dinosaur, as if trying to record the image of this great engine on the baby's mind just as surely as those with cameras were doing with tape and film.

A good part of our route paralleled highways, and I wondered that no one died as a consequence of our passing. Cars raced along beside us, microphones and cameras hanging out doors and windows, in some cases men clinging to the tops of vehicles with one hand and running a camera with the other. I suppose this wouldn't have been all that dangerous, but these racing, preoccupied drivers were confronting other drivers going the other way, people shocked to encounter the speeding mass of traffic—and that mighty engine 50 yards away on the rail tracks! Horns honked, tires squealed.

Izzy, fearless as ever, had me hold his right arm while he leaned out the left side of the engine as far as possible to capture the churning drivers and wheels of the engine. For a while I thought he might fall and die, but then I thought, what the hell—I can't think of a better way to die, and probably Izzy can't either, unless it would be some mysterious Oriental process involving the waitress at the Yen Ching.

Stops Along the Way

The train stopped occasionally along the route to show off the engine, and to let the various politicians and commercial hustlers in the cars behind the engine step out onto depot platforms and blather. Of course, no one cared about them. Politicians and hustlers are silly enough to begin with; imagine how utterly effete they looked alongside that engine! Everyone at the depots looked past the speakers, mouths open, eyes unblinking at that engine. No one heard a word; all ears were tuned to the timpani rumble of the mighty engine.

My favorite stop (I can't recall what town it was) was at a place where the engine had to roll a couple hundred feet past the depot so the officials and dignitaries could disembark and do what they could to steal the scene. I was looking out the other side of the engine at what was obviously a school class, maybe 30 fifth-graders, all sitting in a row along a loading dock, staring at that engine. Just staring and listening and smelling. If adults lose their senses in the company of #3985, well, children . . . I don't know where their minds go.

The engineer had let me blow the whistle a few times, so I knew which cord to pull. He was busy answering questions from a local reporter who had entered the engine at the stop, so I tapped him on the shoulder, made a questioning face, and pulled as if tugging at the whistle cord. I pointed out the window, and pointed back at myself, again making the whistle motion. He nodded yes.

Izzy focused his camera on the kids. I reached over and pulled the cord. The whistle shrieked. In a thousand years I couldn't have anticipated the result. In absolute synchronization, as if blown down by a hurricane, all two dozen of those kids fell over sideways. Izzy was so startled he almost lost the shot.

Izzy with his camera, and Bud in the editing room can make the dull seem interesting, the modest impressive, the mundane special. But we knew there was no way we were going to capture Engine #3985 for the television screen. Can't be done. It's like having a Brownie camera at the Grand Canyon: a waste of film.

But when we watched our footage of the engine in full roar, white and black smoke pouring from her, the drivers churning like the knees and elbows of an Olympic runner, we knew. We knew. Engine #3985 is not a machine. It's alive.

Kids

I'm not very enthusiastic about children. Oh, my four are okay. In fact, they're great. It's other people's kids I don't like very much. Despite my aversion, however, it has been impossible to report on the status of small-town and rural America without referring now and then to children. I hate to admit it but I suspect that my uneasiness with kids is that I know them too well, and know that they know me—which is to say us adults—too well. Kids won't put up with artifice, image, acting, style, pretense, performance, or diplomacy. They're too honest.

The Postcards we've done about children have proven to be favorites with "Sunday Morning's" audience, however, and they have also been some of the easiest ones we've done. Because children don't put up with artifice, image, acting, style, pretense, diplomacy. Sure, there are always the few who put on the shy child act but most of the time children have no trouble at all dealing with cameras, lights, and microphones.

Rich and Jeri Fries's kids had no problems with our presence when we did the story about what it means to grow up on a farm because they were so busy doing their usual farm chores they didn't have time to make much accommodation for a CBS crew. Moreover, we were on their turf—the barn, the fields, a tractor cab, home plate. If anything, we were the ones likely to feel uncomfortable.

Same with our story about detasslers. I won't go into the technology of gene engineering, but in order to permit control of which corn plant mates with which corn plant in a gigantic field (a full mile on each side), in which seed corn is being generated, the tassel (the male part of the plant) of each and every cornstalk (all million or so of them), has to be pulled off. And it is teenage detasslers who do that enormous, grinding task every year.

Each morning for several weeks, youngsters all across the Great Plains roll out of bed about 3 a.m., and trudge to a meeting place where other kids are waiting, and get in an uncomfortable, rented school bus. Then they bump along for an hour or so, go back out into the cold morning air—the sun is still not up—and begin a long day of slogging through irrigation-water-filled rows of corn, no level step for hours on end, and get slashed by razor-edge corn leaves. They must reach high above their heads to jerk up on the tassel to tear it free of the plant. Then, at the end of the long day, they get back on the bus and bounce back home for an hour or so. It's not easy work.

Nor is it slavery. Kids compete for the job around here. It's very good money for a relatively short-term job. They work with friends. There's not a lot of time for socializing, what with being sleepy in the morning, busy during the day, and exhausted by afternoon, but you'd be surprised how often those kids get off the bus singing, laughing, or at the edge of launching into a water fight.

My Postcard was about agriculture and the importance of young people to it in America, but the letters I got suggest it was also a story about what America needs. I got piles of mail from viewers wishing every kid in America could have a chance to go detassling just once in their lifetimes, to realize the good feeling of a hard day's work well done, to enjoy a check that is a matter of merit, not charity, to understand the taste of clean air, cold water, hot sweat, responsibility, respect, and good fellowship. I feel the same way, so those were the viewer letters I could easily understand and fully enjoy.

Rural School Buses

We did another story about school buses. I wanted to show how the rhythms of a day go in the rural countryside. I thought I'd show how my own days are bracketed by the arrival of the school bus to pick up Antonia for school in the morning, and its return late in the afternoon to bring her home. But showing the function of the school bus in our lives also meant, well, showing the school bus.

I grew up in a small city. I never rode a school bus in my entire life. So I had visions of these things as being rolling mayhem, moving riots, hell on wheels. I envisioned fights, things being thrown, sick kids, people hanging out the windows, sheer hell.

Well, that's not the way it is. People being people, especially farm people being farm people, they develop strategies to deal with such potentials. In reality, school buses out this way are models of decorum. Sue Halsey, an old friend of ours, is one of Dannebrog's school drivers. When she drives, she brings along a good book. If there is any trouble at all in her bus, she issues a warning. If the trouble persists, she pulls over, stops the bus, and reads a couple pages to herself. The children, anticipating a world of trouble if they arrive late to school and agonizing about losing precious minutes of freedom if they get home late, quiet down pretty quickly. Usually. If not, Sue just reads another couple pages.

Same with Iola Torres, another friend, neighbor, and school bus driver. If her passengers give her trouble, she warns first and then issues citations for the problem passengers to come to her house and wash the bus. The next Saturday. Have you ever washed a bus? If the kids don't bother to show up, they don't have a ride the next week. Can you imagine telling your parents that, uh, you won't be riding the bus the next five days, that, er, they'll have to get out of bed and drive you the 10 miles to school and pick you up again that afternoon to bring you home? No matter how irresponsible the parents, I think that probably gets their attention.

Naming Children

We did one Postcard directly in school, in my daughter's classroom. I wanted to make some noise about one of my pet peeves, the annoying new custom of naming children with thoroughly goofy, utterly meaningless names.

I mean, good grief—naming a kid is one of the biggest responsibilities anyone can have. This is something another human being is going to have to live with for the better part of a century, long after you're gone. But all too many oh-so-moderns think they're giving a name to a child. Nothing could be further from the truth. The person you are naming will be a child a couple years, then an adolescent a couple more, and then an adult for, oh, 60 or 70 years. With a name like Justun, or Hether, or Jerad, or Brandee. The presumption seems to be, this kid will never be president of a local Rotary Club let alone the United States, so let's give him/her a silly name that would be more appropriate for a dog or a cat or a rowboat than an adult human being. It's a cruelty that deserves substantial punishment in my estimation.

I consider myself a victim of that abuse. "Roger" and "Lee" have nothing to do with anything. They are names picked out of a name book. I get the feeling that no one in the family wanted me named after them. Or maybe that my folks didn't want to take a chance.

I think we need more flexibility with our names. I have changed mine to Roger Lee-Flack Welsch to reflect my love, admiration, and respect for my mother's family. When I was adopted into the Omaha Tribe I was given the name Tenuga Gahi, or Bull Buffalo Chief, a name I bear with enormous pride.

I may have other names: I once mentioned in a German literature class I was teaching that I always admired the poetess Annette von Droste-Huelshof for her splendid name if not her poetry. I made some point to my class about my own wish that somewhere down the

27

line I might get a name with a hyphen in it. To my amazement, a student sitting in the back row, who had not said much at all during the entire semester, raised his hand. I called on him.

"Professor Welsch," he said with some seriousness. "Does son of a bitch have a hyphen in it?"

I gave him an "A" for the semester.

Our daughter is Antonia (two great-grandmothers and a major Plains literary figure) Emily (a grandmother and a sister) Celestine (grandmother) Welsch (a long history of one side of her proud heritage raping and pillaging the other side of her proud heritage for millennia). Now, that is naming with an eye on tradition!

Anyway, we went to Centura school where we shot a classroom, coat rack, desks, and bulletin boards full of Jessikas, Ashlees, Tylors, Krystuls, Keelies, Bambees, and Trishas. My bet is that every one of them will, upon reaching their majority, change their names. I also predict that 20 years from now an enormous proportion of Americans will be known to others by their initials, B. E. being one hell of a lot more dignified for a CEO or state governor—maybe even a plumber or ditch digger—than Brandan Eyan.

It was a good story, even though I know I made a few new enemies. Antonia Emily Celestine, for example. She made it clear that there would never again be a circumstance when I would be permitted to shoot a story about her classmates that would then appear on television where each of them could see their names held up to ridicule.

Okay. So it was a little miscalculation.

Christmas Pageant

Your most popular children's Postcard was also mine, a relatively simple story about a straightforward school Christmas program. The charm of the story was that it was a very small school; a total of three students in one room. And these three kids performed for a little better than an hour, entertaining nearly 100 friends, neighbors, and kin, with poise, charm, good humor, and confidence. They sang, acted, hosted, welcomed, served, and got a standing ovation at the end of the evening.

The sad part of the story never made it to the Postcard as it finally aired. Within two years of our airing the Christmas pageant, the teacher, Linda's aunt, Helen Horacek, retired. The school board closed the school, sold the building, and moved it away, leaving little to remind anyone of that magical evening. I imagine that the children of that district now attend a much bigger school with much more modern equipment. I can't help but wonder how much better an education they receive.

Festival

I suppose it's not surprising that since people love festivals, people also like television stories about festivals. And festivals do make good television stories: there is almost always plenty of color, music, food, laughter, dance, history, tradition, family; all the things people consider good and important. Even when there is suspicion, uneasiness, or anger aimed at an ethnic, religious, or racial group, everyone feels welcome and comfortable when that community opens its doors in festival. I suppose that's the secret—it's a matter of opening a door.

Of course there are plenty of celebrations that are first and fundamentally in-group observations. For example, I participate in some religious ceremonies within the Omaha Indian Tribe, just about the most hospitable community in America (as Lewis and Clark attest from their visit in 1804!) that are, if not private, not precisely public.

When I first began spending time among the Omaha 35 years ago, I began to hear veiled references to "prayer meetings," and I thought they might be interesting ceremonies to observe. It's not polite within the Omaha culture to ask questions, certainly not to invite oneself into things like, uh, a prayer meeting, but I did, and my friends within the tribe dealt with it well, being used to dealing with the abrasive and sometimes downright rude behavior of the white man.

But I never managed to get to a meeting. I either just missed one or none was planned or . . . well, whatever was going on, something was always going on. That was the pattern for many years. Then, in 1967, I was adopted into the tribe and given my Omaha name, Tenuga Gahi, Bull Buffalo Chief. I had the good fortune the night of my adoption ceremony in Macy, Nebraska, the tribal agency town, to have a flat tire on my pickup truck. That's right: good fortune.

As I sat on the curb changing it, my new brother Alfred "Buddy" Gilpin Jr., sat with me, telling me about my new obligations, responsibilities and privileges. This was the first indication I had that I hadn't just been given an honorary name, but had actually become a blood Omaha, as much his brother as if we had been born to the same mother.

Buddy asked me if there was anything he could help me with in understanding my new situation and I mentioned that, well, if the occasion ever came up, I sure would like to attend a prayer meeting. "Ah, yes," he said, and told me that not only did he know about prayer meetings, he conducted them, that he "had a fireplace," and was ordained to conduct services in the Native American Church. And of course, as his brother, I would be welcome. Although, he warned me, it is not an easy church service to attend: for one thing, a prayer meeting begins at sundown, and goes on until sunup. One sits flat on the ground, not rising from our Mother Earth all night long, without sleeping. This is in a tipi, where there are no solid, straight walls to lean on.

I explained that whatever the rigors, I felt strongly enough about the Omaha people and my new association with them that I would like to go to a meeting. And I wondered if one would be taking place yet that year. "Listen," he said, with a laugh, lifting his ear to the night sky. And I heard the faint sounds of a drum and high-pitched singing somewhere off to the west of us. "That's one now."

"And there . . ." He turned to the north, from where another song was just beginning. The fact of the matter is, there is rarely a weekend when a prayer meeting is not going on in the Omaha Reservation. Or two. They are not, however, open to the public.

A Great Greek Celebration

Even when festivals are public, they are inevitably to some degree private. About the closest we came to taking a "Sunday Morning" audience into a closed festival of that sort was the time we went to the Bridgeport, Nebraska, Greek Festival. As is the case with the Omaha, the Greeks of Nebraska have some reason to keep to themselves: a mob was lynching Greeks in Omaha as late as 1909! A group under that kind of threat doesn't go out of its way to invite outsiders to its gatherings.

But I had been to the Greek festival in far western Nebraska before and knew that, while history dictated privacy for the Greek community in the Nebraska panhandle, tradition recommended hospitality. In fact, it is precisely the fact that the Bridgeport Greek picnic is an esoteric gathering which appeals to me; this is not an event put on to charm outsiders and fleece tourists. No, this is an occasion for the area's Greeks to fleece the area's Greeks. Whatever deception is going on, is self-deception, good-hearted performance, thoroughly innocent fraud. Although the bilking is done all in good spirit. The picnic is a fund-raising benefit, after all, for the community's church.

I am not using overblown diction here. The first time I went to the Greek gathering, my ears perked up when I heard that some homemade quilts were going to be auctioned. I love and collect quilts. This might be a great chance to pick up some folk art bargains, I thought. Yeah, sure!

The quilts were made by the women of the church specifically for this event and purpose, with all proceeds going to the church. So the first lovely quilt was held up and the auctioneer started his bidding. At $500. But not for long, because the bid soared to over a thousand. And then two. Finally, the bidding ended and the hammer came down on a price that would have bought a nice car elsewhere.

And the buyer was—the lady's husband. Who wanted to be sure that his wife's handiwork was appraised at an appropriately inflated level! And after he picked up his new quilt and showed it off as if he'd just captured a prize, he gave it back to the auctioneer to go on the block again. And the quilt was sold again, at a slightly lower but still obscene price, to one of the woman's brothers. And so it went, with quilt after quilt being multiply sold, leaving the church wealthy, the women and their husbands suitably proud, and us few outsiders gasping for breath and scratching itches we'd been afraid to address when the bids were flying.

But another form of folk art was available at the Bridgeport festival at a much more accessible price, mercifully—food. Baklava, cabbage rolls, gyros, souvlaki, roast lamb, breads, pastries, all washed down with generous quantities of retsina and ouzo. And the music . . .

The first few times I went to the festival there was a live band, from Denver, but later, as traditional musicians became ever harder to find, there were recordings and audio tapes. A shame to be sure, but the dancing was still electric, and I bemoaned my German-ness as black-eyed girls flirted and beckoned to those of us seated at the dining tables, luring us onto the dancing platform, where we could drop ever more cash into the church's box in the center of the floor! "Make a joyful noise . . ." indeed!

There were other festivals for "Sunday Morning" Postcards too—an Omaha powwow with swirling feathers and ancient tribal music and good food—fry bread and corn soup, for example. A Danish Independence Day festival in Dannebrog with rullapols, kringele, and akavit, an antique tractor show, a county fair, a corn picking contest.

The Circus Comes to Town

A quieter but nonetheless traditional festival I especially enjoyed sending by way of a Postcard was the coming of the Plunkett Family

Circus to Dannebrog, a real adventure into the past for me. When I was a young boy, there wasn't a lot of money around. My parents were laborers to begin with, but there was also the Depression, and then World War Two; not much money for frivolous things.

So, when the circus came to Lincoln, Nebraska, if I got to go, it was on the basis of a free school ticket, which insured us only a place under the tent. A couple times I asked Dad if we could go to the circus for real, like my buddy Billy Danek, but there wasn't the money. And as if that weren't enough, Dad, trying to make it better, made it even worse by rousting me out of bed before dawn to take me down to the big pasture just west of the Gooch's Mill so I could see the circus train pull in and unload. Dad, this is not the circus!

Only later would I realize that what I witnessed in those dawn hours was better than the circus my financially better-endowed friends were seeing later in the day. I watched elephants pull wagons around and raise the big top; I saw workers—who later in the day became clowns and trapeze artists—slamming great mauls onto tent stakes rapid-fire, as if there were a high-speed steam ram driving them; I saw beautiful acrobats practicing a lot closer than Billy Danek ever got to enjoy. And I accumulated memories much better than those all of the other Lincoln kids whose parents had the wherewithal to take them to the real circus.

So, when I heard it was possible a small circus would be coming to Dannebrog, I knew that this was my chance to renew wonderful memories, and it was.

Once again I got to watch the elephants unload and raise a tent. I saw circus performers put together their equipment and challenge the forces of gravity right there on the Dannebrog softball diamond, right where my daughter Antonia had played first base the evening before. Sure, this time there were only a handful of performers, and two elephants, and a couple of high-flying beauties, but it was enough to reignite thousands of tired synapses in my aging mind.

The performance was wonderful, the parade down the main street of town was magic. The weather was perfect. It couldn't have been a better day, and what's more, I had the feeling that it was just as special a day for the Plunkett Family as it was for Dannebrog.

I thought it was a joke when I first heard it, as I watched a family of trampoline acrobats practice. On further consideration, I decided it wasn't a joke at all when one of the performers scolded his young son for losing focus while practicing his routine: "Now, shape up and fly right, my boy . . . or I'll make you run away and join the town."

Pickup Trucks

A lot has been made of America's alleged love affair with automobiles. Frankly, that particular romance has never been a part of my fantasies. I don't believe it is true of most Americans, who go, after all, to demolition derbies to see cars purposely destroyed.

About the closest I've ever felt to a car I've owned is to think it's all right, or maybe not too bad. I don't recall ever changing the oil in a car. I have never opened a car hood idly—only in despair. I laugh in the face of those who think an automobile is an investment. I can't even take cars seriously as transportation: I would at the snap of a finger surrender the "freedom" of the financial stupidity, grinding boredom, and immediate hazards of driving a car for a decent American railway system.

But it's true that I am nonetheless a gearhead. I write about old tractors, rebuild old tractors, spend every moment of leisure up to my elbows in a filthy old tractor engine, and find my happiest moments in my shop working on old tractors. You already know that some of my finest moments in life were the hours I stood in the cab of the great steam engine known coldly as UP #3985 only by those who don't understand. And soon you will hear about the time I actually got to take the stick of a Fighting Falcon F-16. I have driven race cars as fast as my nerves would handle. I can talk engines and tractors endlessly.

But not cars. They bore me, and the newer they are, the more boring they seem to be.

Which is not to say I haven't had my share of automotive concerns during the tenure of Postcards from Nebraska with "Sunday Morning." I can't even count the number of letters I've received expressing, briefly, the heated opinion, "If you're so damned proud of America and American workers and American culture, why were you driving a Jap (or German, or Swedish, or English) automobile in your last segment, you fat, overalled idiot?!"

On a few—very few—occasions the complainers were right.

Sort of. If we were out on a shoot somewhere and a shot was needed of me driving, there were times when Producer Bud might say, "Rog, jump into the car and drive by Iz's camera," or "We need a driving shot; Iz, get into the car with Rog and get him driving by the building . . ." And I would get into the car—the rental car we happened to be driving, which likely as not was an import—and I would do my on-camera work.

For my own part, in our vehicular stable we have maybe 30 tractors, all clearly of American manufacture, and three family vehicles. A Ford Taurus, Linda's Ford Ranger pickup truck, and my own battered Ford F-150, the Blue Beast, which has appeared in a couple dozen Postcards (and before that, Blue Thunder, an even older and even more battered example of the same model).

Our Ford Taurus is a good car. I do like it. It is comfortable and efficient and handsome. I don't love it, but, okay, I like it.

Linda's pickup is what my mother refers to, a reference I cited in my Postcard about pickups, as "one of those cute little trucks." In it I feel like I'm driving a riding mower: it is too small, too shiny, too pretty, too sissy. It is more like a car than a truck, and therefore more like a pain in the butt than a useful tool. But Linda likes it, and it's hers, and I don't drive it unless I have to.

My Ford F-150 pickup truck is another issue. It might be pushing the point to say I love it, but I do like it. Okay, I'm fond of it. Like most things all of us like, I like it insofar as it is like me; not handsome but rugged, oblivious to pain or vanity, strong, noisy, disreputable, a little on the stinky side. I am comfortable in the cab of the Blue Beast. I don't need to worry about dirt on my overalls or mud on my boots when I get in it. I don't have to lock it when I leave it sitting on Main Street. I can drive across open fields and pastures without worrying about cedar branches scratching its paint or rocks denting the fenders.

I once squeaked between a couple trees and tore off the side-view mirrors. Solution? Get two new side-view mirrors. I throw old iron or dead calves into the bed of the truck without concern. Antonia and I drive it up to the uplands and sleep in the back overnight so we can see the Perseids meteor showers. The truck is not a prize or asset; it's a tool. It's a friend.

No wonder that one of the most popular Postcards I ever sent to America via "Sunday Morning" was the one about rural pickup trucks. It is a curiosity to me that people who recognize me in airports or restaurants, viewers who want to tell me their favorite Postcards, are so utterly predictable. Some like the very first reports I did (on overalls, or even later ones like the smokehouse piece). But by far and away, the most common praise is for that one we did in the very first years of the series, before we really knew what our Postcards were going to look like in the long-run, the one about pickup trucks.

The Essence of the Pickup

I think that popularity is because we said some things only pickup truck owners and rural people understand—what a pickup truck really is. It's not just another vehicle. The thesis of my Postcard was that pickup trucks are not what they are said to be on television commercials. They are not my mother's "cute little trucks." They are not shiny, they are not simply practical (although they are that), they are not economical (they *eat* gas!), they are not convenient for delivering the family. If they offer some of those things, okay, but that is not what the pickup means to most owners.

This was not the sort of Postcard Bud likes to do. In fact, he was initially very skeptical. "Rog, you see these examples of trucks every day, over months and years of time. How are we supposed to find them all in the one day we have to shoot the piece? Can we drive down the main streets of three towns within 30 minutes of here and see what you're talking about? You write here about pickups with pliers for door handles, and with corn growing three feet high in the bed. Are we going to see that *today?* If not, we're moving on."

I assured him we would find enough examples, even though I was fairly sure we wouldn't. It's not that the examples weren't here, it's just that like most things in life, they weren't likely to be there when we needed them. Last week? Of course! Next week? Sure. Today? Probably not.

And we didn't find all that we wanted or exactly what we needed, but we found enough. We found a pickup truck in Boelus's filling station, 10 miles from Dannebrog, with at least 100 wadded up cigarette pack wrappers piled on the dash. And a bed full of unidentifiable scrap iron. We found another in Dannebrog (someone in town just to pick up the mail) with some ancient corn kernels sprouting in the bed. My buddy Bondo drifted through town with his truck that only starts if you sit toward the middle of the seat, press the brake halfway down, and turn the key as hard as you can counter-clockwise.

We found Gale Smith in town with his truck that has a Vise-Grip pliers for a door handle, and another (I don't recall whose) with a length of barbed wire replacing the radio antenna. ("Brings in country music better," said the owner, straight-faced.) We got shots of a truck with a distinct lean to the left from the constant overload of its owner in the driver's seat, and one with bungee cords holding down the hood.

There was no shortage of trucks with carpenter's levels in the rifle racks, and of course there were plenty with rifles in the back window.

In Grand Island we got shots of the enormous (and enormously silly) monster trucks with huge tires and shiny bodies; not at all pickup trucks but power icons. And at a dealer's lot we got some of those new "cute little trucks your wife won't be at all embarrassed to drive to the grocery store."

That too is more a consideration than it might seem. One of the major benefits of The Blue Beast is that when Antonia needs a ride to volleyball practice after school or retrieval from a Halloween dance at one in the morning, and I volunteer, she asks me what vehicle I'm driving. I answer, "Blue Beast," she declines—making her embarrassment clear and paramount, and Linda winds up having to drive her "cute little truck" instead. At those moments when Antonia wavers, I add ". . . But I have a load of old iron . . ." or, "I'll come get you right after I pick up some dead calves over at Leos' . . . ," and the response is instantaneous: "Let me talk with Mom."

A good pickup truck is like an old chore coat, with cookie crumbs, a few washers, and some drywall screws in the pocket. Or like old boots, scarred, scraped, and scuffed, but as comfortable as, well, as an old shoe. And a good part of that comfort is that a *real* pickup truck is not a source of worry in one's life. It sits outside in the snow and sun because it doesn't make any difference if the finish is a little dull and the bed a little rusty. A *real* pickup truck is a vehicle you can stand on at the kid's softball game. You may wash a *real* pickup truck, but you never polish it.

A *real* pickup truck is the only vehicle left in your garage, or in your life, that has a name.

Overalls

For all the citified folks who consider my overalls an assault on their sophistication, there is another, substantial group of "Sunday Morning" viewers who recognize my garb as

1) a reflection of an authentic American folk costume;
2) the most comfortable possible ensemble for the broad conditions under which we have worked over our 10 years in the field;
3) entirely appropriate to Nebraska's agricultural heritage; and
4) an explicit expression of my genuine contempt for the goofy notion that the substance of people can be judged by the clothes they wear.

I feel particularly strong about that fourth category. My grandparents were migrant sugar beet laborers; my parents were laborers and domestics; the same goes for my in-laws, whom I love very much. I know they are all wonderfully honorable, well- (if self-) educated people. I know that I have met few people in overalls who aren't damn fine folks; and I know I have met a lot of people in expensive, fancy suits who are first-class, industrial-grade bastards and crooks.

So, I wear overalls. To be specific, I wear Key Imperial overalls, made in Fort Scott, Kansas, proudly labeled "The Aristocrat of Overalls." I like to joke that this is why I wear them, because I consider myself to be an aristocrat of overall wearers. Actually, I wear Keys because I think they're the most comfortable, best wearing, best designed overalls I've found (although I also like Pointers and Big Smiths).

I like the notion of a flap covering one of the bib pockets. I also liked the low-backed model, with fancy, crossed, elastic suspenders, but they quit making them a few years ago, underscoring Eric's Law: "If you find something you like, buy a lifetime supply because they're just about to quit making them."

I started wearing overalls when I first began teaching at the University of Nebraska in 1973. I don't even remember why. Or where or when I bought my first ones. I suspect it was a part of my conscious joining of the hippie movement, an era whose passing I painfully lament.

I still love the idea that students in those halcyon days learned what they thought would be interesting to learn rather than what would make them a dollar, for example. I loved their willingness to be curious and enthusiastic.

I reject George Wills' idiotic contention—one of his many idiotic contentions, we might note—that it was the hippies who gave us the violence and excesses of the current drug plague. That terror came to us courtesy of his favorites; unrestrained capitalists who developed ever-better [read: worse] drugs with ever-greater [read: murderous] economic potential and competition, not to mention an arrogance and self-righteousness precisely of George Wills' usual and sorry sort. I'm glad ABC has him. Serves 'em right.

The Lore and Lowdown

Anyway, it was also about that time that I acquired my Danne-brog property and got to know real farmers who wore (and often still wear) overalls as a part of their daily garb. It was also about that time that I began to notice the protocol and ethnology of overalls, a factor that very much attracted me, anthropologist that I am.

I watched the utility of overalls well beyond their designers' intentions: rolled cuffs serving as emergency ashtrays, bibs making windbreaks for lighting pipes and cigarettes. Removed from the wearer, they can replace towropes to pull cars out of mud holes, the legs of the overalls tied around one bumper, the suspenders around the other.

I learned the folklore of this bit of Americana. A twisted strap averts lightning strikes, both side buttons are done up for formal wear, all four are left open for the ventilation called for in-field work. (Underwear is reserved for receptions at the Lincoln Center or audiences with the Pope!)

I learned the literature of overalls. It was one of good ol' Bumps Nielsen's favorites about the three Danes bragging about their respective abilities in digging holes for local outhouses:

Dane #1: "Me, by gollies, I digs a hole, working at it all morning, and den I moves de outhouse over dat hole, and den to test it I sits down and I poops. And I counts 'One . . . two . . . tree . . .' and den, by gollies, it hits de bottom. Dat's how good I digs 'em."

Dane #2: "Me, by gollies, I digs a hole, working at it all day, and den I moves de outhouse over dat hole, and den to test it, I sits down and I poops. And I counts 'One . . . two . . . tree . . . ten . . . tventy . . .

hunnert . . .' and den, by gollies, it hits de bottom. Dat's how good I digs 'em."

Dane #3: "Me, by gollies, I digs a hole, working at it a week and a half and den I moves de outhouse over dat hole, and den to test it, I sits down and I poops. And I counts 'One . . . two . . . tree . . . ten . . . twenty . . . hunnert . . . six hunnert . . . nine hunnert and twenty-tree . . .' and den, by gollies, I looks down dat hole and der she is, hung up in dem overalls straps just like always!"

I do wear overalls every day here on the farm and most of the time when I travel, for all of the above reasons. And, at the urging of many of my viewers, I have considered developing a line of Roger Welsch designer overalls. You know, Spandex running overalls, maybe some Speedo swimming overalls, and of course, velour lounging overalls. My buddies in town tell me that America may not be ready yet for a Roger Welsch line of overalls. And they may be right.

ADDRESS

MP

My Favorite
Postcards from
Nebraska

Harvest

I imagine that anyone watching the Postcards from Nebraska with any regularity and care would have noticed that they were loaded a little heavy on the harvest side. We sent Postcards on all manner of crops; apples and beef, grain elevators and gasohol. And we covered agriculture from the bizarre—salmon, ostriches, and herd dogs—to the ordinary; children growing up within farm families to become farmers themselves, youngsters doing their part for agriculture by working as detasslers in seed corn fields. But just as harvest and its hope dominate any rural countryside, they were also the focus of a substantial number of our essays.

My own interest in harvest began long before I lived on rural ground, before I was ever sending Postcards. When I first met Charles Kuralt, in fact, back in the early 1970s, I included in my "Kuralt File" a note about "moon machines." My contention has always been that if extra-terrestrial aliens really took a notion to invade Planet Earth, the ideal time to do it would be harvest, when a good part of our population has its attention focused elsewhere. Then the invaders could drive great, hulking, lurching war machines up and down the highways with little more notice than an occasional grumpy honk from city folks who don't know any better.

I've heard stories in the wine country of Germany that during World War II, when the Allies were entering Hitler's Reich through the east-west corridor of the Mosel Valley, vineyard owners there refused to make way for military vehicles and personnel because, as they quite reasonably argued, grapes when they are ready are *ready*, just as they had been for millenia before. While war can be fought just about any time, as wars had been, after all, for millenia before. It is not an accident (and it is one of my favorite bits of rural diction), that harvest is often referred to as a "campaign," a recognition of the basically military, highly technological, severely demanding rigors of that farming season.

Understanding the urgency in getting all that food to the bins, barns, sheds, elevators, tanks, silos, and processors in such a short window of time, I gladly—even gleefully—wave at farmers negotiating the highways and fields in their harvest machines, no matter what the haste of my own errands. "Don't mind me," I think as I join the long lines behind the combines, pickers, wagons, and tractors on Plains highways. "I can get to Omaha anytime. The corn needs to be picked RIGHT NOW."

As harvest gains momentum, as the grain reaches the proper stage of ripeness, hardness, and dryness in more and more fields, as fall deepens and winter threatens, the mystery and furor of the process extends well past sundown, and then the magic gains a new dimension. Even when there are no "moon machines" slowing traffic on the roads and highways, as we plunge through Nebraska nights we see the great machines, festooned with lights, haloed in dust clouds, lurching through the fields, later and later . . . until suddenly there are no more. The harvest is over, just like that, and the machines have gone back to whatever planet they came from in the first place.

And then the flatlands are freckled with yellow and brown mountains of grain, waiting for railcars to move them to cover and processing elsewhere. Streets in towns are mounded high with grain. It becomes hard for those of us who don't understand precisely what is going on to see how all of this stuff is ever going to be cleaned up and carried away.

Catching the Action

Before Kuralt could bring his own golden prose to those scenes, however, I began my Postcards from Nebraska, and I got to tell that story. We shot footage of all those things; machinery on the highway, tractors in the fields, piles of grain, elevators filling, railcars loading.

The best part for me was late one night, however, in a field midway between Central City and my place at Dannebrog. We scouted the fields, trying to find a good place to park the car, to enter a field, to approach one of the farmers at work harvesting. It was a pitch-black night, but all around us, spotted one to a field, we could see the bright lights of combines and corn pickers at work. Trucks and tractors stood ready to take the grain to shelter. Cars of weary farm wives and children were bringing food and drink to the men and women in the harvest machines.

The air was filled with the roar of great engines and the ripping of stalks and stems; everywhere there was the smell of dust, dirt, exhaust, grain, and dry foliage. We parked the car, grabbed the camera, tripod, sound equipment, lights, batteries, and tapes (even "the star" and producer are pack animals when it comes to a shoot like this one). We made our way out into a field, through the dry corn-stalks, toward the breaking point between the tall, unpicked corn and the savaged ground where the picker had already wrenched the grain from the stalk, ripping it off the husk, rasping the grain from the cob, and then spitting the refuse out behind it while tucking away the pre-cious grain in its mobile hopper.

We could see the picking machine a quarter-mile away at the other end of the field, just now turning around to come back at us down the long rows. We set up the lights and the camera so we could catch my script reading just as the machine would pass behind me.

Minutes later, the roar and dust almost burying us, the machine's lights fell on us, standing off to the side on the picked ground. We waved down the farmer, realizing that it was dangerous being out in front of that machine, especially so late in the day when the operator was exhausted and battered from a long day's dirty, tedious work—perhaps a long week's "campaign." We knew we had to explain our errand fast and get out of his way.

He stopped the great machine and threw open his door. I climbed up the ladder to the cab and explained to his dust-lined face and bleary eyes, "We're from CBS News, doing a story on harvest. Would it be okay if we turn on our lights and shoot some pictures of you as you finish this last row?"

He looked at me as if I were some sort of apparition. Small wonder. He might have been driving combines through these fields every fall almost all his life and never once come across another human being out here in the middle of nowhere, let alone a camera crew from CBS News! "Yeah, sure," he said. "Sorry I can't stop to talk but they're talking about rain for tomorrow."

"Right. We'll stay out of your way. Good luck. Good harvest," I said, and climbed back down his machine's ladder. I could hear the gears shift in the great transmission, the engine pick up speed, and once again the machine and its pilot slashed into the harvest.

We returned to the van with all our equipment and closed down for the night. I think we wound up at Dreisbach's Steak House in Grand Island for supper late that evening. And I think we all ate our meal with a special thought of gratitude to that guy still out there in the cab of his cornpicker, still bringing in the sheaves while we were enjoying the bounty of his work.

Real Farming

I have always been interested, however, not simply in the tech-nology and industry of harvest but also in its human dimension. My

45

farm is a tree farm, mostly a hobby. I plant trees, do some pruning and watering, cut a little firewood. But it's not the same as real farming.

When I lose some of my trees to hail or storm or fire or insects, I anguish and lament, but it's not the same as real farming. When my friends who are really farmers lose a crop, after all, it may mean that the wife doesn't get the operation she needs, or that one of the kids doesn't go to college this year, or—in the very worst cases—that the farm that's been in the family since it was homesteaded by a great-great-grandfather more than a century and a half ago will be lost forever. That's real farming.

And real farming requires a spirit, understanding, and mentality I just don't have. I have told the story a thousand times, and I'm going to tell it to you here again. I was once driving over to the Golden Nugget Steak House in Boelus, just 10 miles west of my place, for a couple cold beers and supper one day, when I met coming toward me my friend Marv Casperson, driving his big grain truck. I could see it was full of corn. He was, I reasoned, heading toward the grain elevator in one of the next towns, maybe Grand Island, to sell his harvest. Right behind him was his wife Marlene, driving another truck, and one of their sons in a truck behind them. No doubt about it—they were hauling a part of the harvest to market.

I waved to them and drove on, wondering what it must be like to be a real farmer, facing all the hazards of bringing in a crop—wind, hail, drought, fire, bugs, cold, heat, whatever—and then finally one day facing victory, the bringing in of the crop in defiance of all those perils. Well, I was pretty sure that the Caspersons would be coming into the Nugget for supper (at least a celebratory drink) after they finished dumping the grain, so I resolved to hang around until they got back and just ask them myself.

They came in much later that evening, but I was still waiting. I sat down with them, ordered a round of beers, and asked them my goofy question: "Now, you guys know I'm not a real farmer, but I'm interested in what it must be like to be a farmer. So, what does it feel like when you've done all the work, got around all the problems, faced all the hazards, dodged all the disasters, and you actually bring in the crop and take it to market like you just did?"

They all looked at me a moment, a little surprised I'm sure to hear a question like this that they'd never heard (or for that matter thought of) before. And then Marv said as if he'd rehearsed it, "Haven't cashed the check yet."

I regathered my wits. "Well, okay, but once you cash the check, what will it feel like?"

"Have to see how we come out after expenses."

"But once you sort all that out . . ."

"Big tractor is stuck in that wet ground down by the creek, and God only knows what kind of damage we might do to it or my other tractor pulling it out."

The moral of that evening was that no farmer can ever afford to exercise the hubris of celebrating a harvest unconditionally because the victory is never final, never total, never unequivocal. My appreciation for Marv and his family, for all farmers, and for the harvest increased at that moment's realization by a factor of 10.

Arbor Day

Nebraska is grain country when it comes to crops, but along the eastern-most fringe of the region, within a few miles of the Missouri River and its woodlands, there are orchards too. On one occasion we visited an apple orchard near Nebraska City, all the more appropriate a place to enjoy an arboreal bounty because that town is the home of Arbor Day.

Our story carried a powerful human dimension beyond harvest, however. The subject of our story was a stout farm worker by the name of William Oberdieck, working as he had most of his life at the Kimmel Orchards near Nebraska City.

It would have been enough to carry the story to know that Oberdieck loved his trees, and was virtually a part of the Kimmel Family, for whom he worked. Over the years of his service in the Kimmel trees, the farm had become a part of his legacy, his inheritance too. As he walked among his charges and talked with us about them, he patted them, rubbed their bark, admired their produce. We drank cider from his trees, and ate apple pie. We sat with Oberdieck and the Kimmels and talked about trees.

And we talked about the days when Oberdieck was not a cherished friend of the family, not a respected colleague, but a prisoner, working in the trees as a part of his incarceration, away from his family, away from his homeland. As a young man, Oberdieck was a soldier of the Wehrmacht in North Africa. When Hitler's Afrika Korps collapsed, Oberdieck made his way westward along the northern edge of the continent, was eventually taken captive by the Allies, and shipped to a prison camp in America to wait out the duration of the war. As fate would have it, he was imprisoned in a small prison in central Nebraska.

Oberdieck was an educated man, a man of some pride. He was bored and stifled by prison life, so when an offer was issued for prisoners to do farm work, he volunteered. This was not unusual during the war; I can recall sitting at the supper table, listening to news of the

47

war in Europe, with German prisoners on my Aunt Emma and Uncle Sam's farm near Lingle, Wyoming. I can remember even at the time thinking it peculiar that these decent, hardworking men were precisely the ones my uncles Elzie, Albert, and Al were trying to kill in Europe. And who, it is only fair to note I suppose, were trying to kill them.

Oberdieck eventually wound up in a prison camp in Weeping Water, Nebraska, working days in the Kimmel Orchards, spending his nights behind barbed wire in the prison camp. He worked hard, he came to be friends with the Kimmels, he came to love the trees, and Nebraska.

He told us a powerful story: the day Germany fell, the American camp commander called Oberdieck into his office and told him the news, asking him if he would mind getting some of the more responsible men in his command to guard the camp themselves that night since the Americans wanted to go to town to celebrate their victory. Oberdieck accepted the charge and they guarded themselves that last night. He said his men sat quietly weeping on their bunks that night as they thought of a shattered nation, wasted lives, squandered resources, ruined dreams, lost years, families in jeopardy, familiar, beloved landscapes—not unlike the Nebraska one in which they toiled—laid waste.

Oberdieck was returned to Germany, maintained contact with the Kimmels, and returned as an immigrant and worker. He joined his former captors in nurturing the trees he had worked with originally as a prisoner, adopting the land, in which he had been an enemy, as his own. And through it was the quiet dignity of William Oberdieck. And of his trees.

Widow Harvest

The most notable harvest story we did, to my mind, was one dealing with so sensitive an issue I wondered if we would ever get it done. I don't know that I have ever been as uncomfortable in all the stories we've done before or after. It wasn't a unique story, not even an unusual one, but it was the kind of thing that is almost impossible to capture by way of an essay.

For example, one story I always wanted to cover was our local volunteer fire department. In a town like Dannebrog, population 324, members of our fire department and emergency medical team are our friends and neighbors. The alarm goes off and people leap from businesses, tractors, shops, stores, offices, and homes and race to the firehouse to grab their equipment and go to the aid of their friends and neighbors. Al and LaVon from the service station, Patty from the bank, Carol from the coffee house, Steve from the machine shop, Kerry from the grocery store . . .

A great story, right?

But what are the chances of the film crew being in town, ready to roll, on one of the dozen or so occasions during a year when the volunteers are summoned to a real fire? Almost none. Sometimes when we've been in the area for a protracted period (several days or a week), we've asked for a pager so we could be right on top of whatever happened in terms of an emergency, and could join the department as they rushed to the job. Never happened. And without the action of the volunteers on the job, the story really isn't much of a story.

So, having lived in Nebraska all my 60 years, I knew from ample experience that every harvest season, in 10 or 20 places around the state (perhaps more for all I knew) neighbors gathered together to bring in a harvest for a disabled farmer. Or, in the worst cases, a widowed wife or orphaned children.

I thought this would make a powerful statement about the importance of neighbors out here, of the strength of community, of the power of fellowship and compassion, of the incredibly dangerous nature of farming. But what usually happened is that on those rare occasions when I heard about such cooperative harvests, they were reports of a harvest that had already taken place. Even if I were to get some prior notice of such an effort by neighbors, what were the chances that it would be a time when we'd arranged for the Postcards crew to be here? Since we made such arrangements months in advance, the chances of everything falling into place just right for a story like that were next to zero.

Then I happened to see an article in the Lincoln newspaper like the ones I see every year; a young farmer killed when his tractor rolled over on him, leaving a wife and two children, and a crop in the fields. One of the emergency medical techs on the spot was a neighbor and friend of the family. While discussing the tragedy, she remarked the community would probably have to get together that fall to bring in the crops for the bereaved family. I wrote a letter of condolence to her and to the widow's parents, who were also mentioned in the newspaper item. I was very uneasy, asking to bring a television crew in for a story at this moment of terrible tragedy, but I felt this was also a powerful, positive story, a moment of disaster that brought out the very best in a community, in Americans.

I called and asked the med tech and widow's father to bring the idea to the widow at some moment when she was able to deal with the idea and let me know what she thought. If the story was out of the question, well, it was out of the question. I certainly wasn't going to intrude on this moment of pain for the family and community.

I heard from both the family and the friends that they'd talked with the dead farmer's wife and family and they understood the power of the good message for America behind this terrible moment for them. So, I was able to coordinate a fall trip for the crew with the widow's harvest.

Which makes things sound a lot simpler than they were. Harvest depends on weather, and so does successful video taping. And the condition of the crop is critical and unpredictable. Grain moisture is measured and monitored on an almost hourly basis, watching for the precise, optimum moment for harvest. I checked constantly for crop moisture. I watched weather forecasts nervously. As the weekend set for the crew's arrival—and hopefully for the harvest—approached, the chances for rain wavered. I got directions to the fields to be harvested. The morning of the harvest I got out of bed deep in the night, looking to the sky. It was studded with stars! We were in luck.

The Story Comes Together

Following the careful directions, we made our way over gravel roads into the hilly country north of Seward, Nebraska. We arrived at the designated corner well before sunrise so Izzy could shoot some pictures of the sun rising over the grained fields, ready for picking. We shot our pictures as the sun came up. I began to get nervous all over again.

The work was supposed to begin at 7 o'clock, minutes after sunrise, minutes from now—but we were still totally alone. I had anticipated an army of workers in the fields, a festival of love and friendship. But there was no one.

A pickup truck approached us, slowed, and stopped. The woman driving turned off the engine and walked toward us. She introduced herself as the med tech I had been corresponding with, the woman who had tried to save the crushed farmer, the person who had made all the arrangements for this impending harvest.

I tried to be diplomatic, in part not to embarrass her, in part because I feared her answer: "So, who's going to be here today? How many combines and pickers and trucks, do you suppose?"

"I don't really know," she said calmly.

Uh-oh. This is the person in charge, and she doesn't have any idea who is going to be here. "You don't have a list, maybe, of who'll be here?"

"Nope."

Ouch. I sensed disaster. Bud looked at me with apprehension. I could read his face: "Done it again, huh, Welsch?"

The designated hour approached, only minutes away, and still there was no one here but us and the woman in charge. I tried to find reassurance in the fact that she didn't seem the least bit nervous. And then began the real miracle of the moment, the one I didn't really anticipate or understand up until then. Izzy poked me and pointed to the west, running to set up his camera. A mile or so away was a cornpicker coming down the gravel road toward us.

And when it came down the hill, behind it appeared another. A grain truck approached from the East. Izzy scrambled with his camera. Two more pickers came down the gravel from the north. And two semi-trailer grain trucks from the south. And more trucks and more combines. And grain wagons and tractors. Pickup trucks hauling hot coffee and fresh rolls. And suddenly, what had been a quiet country crossroads in the middle of nowhere was a hub of unbelievable activity. Engines roared, the air was filled with dust.

The problem, I guess, was the difference between what I had expected and what really happened. I imagined all these machines coming in and whoever was in charge directing the drivers to their respective assignments—grain trucks over there, grain wagons along this fence, those two pickers over there, these two here . . . that kind of thing. I expected the participants to stop to express their condolences, to exchange news of the day (or at least a greeting), to assess the task ahead, to accept some gratitude for this enormous kindness they were about to extend the family.

But there was no one "in charge." To my astonishment, the great machines barely slowed down as they left the road and rolled into the fields they'd come to pick. The drivers might flick a hand of recognition in someone's direction, but as often as not they didn't even do that. It wasn't so much a matter of discourtesy or inattention; they were there for business.

An Education in Agriculture

Of course! This is harvest time, not just for the widow and her family, but for everyone. There was no time to spare, no time to be wasted. These people had been harvesting for days and would be at it for many weeks to come. There would be time for condolences at the memorial service in church the next Sunday morning. There would be time for pleasantries in the local coffee shop or tavern that winter, after the harvest was in.

Machines came one after another, over the hills and directly into the fields. Filled pickers pulled up to trucks and emptied their cargo,

51

again without direction or discussion. I felt silly as I explained to myself, "Of course! These people don't need to be told what to do, or figure out what comes next! They know exactly what to do. There is only one thing that comes next. And they're just doing it. They don't need to talk it over, they need to get it done."

And that's what they did. In an explosion of activity that happened almost too fast for Izzy to capture on tape, the huge fields were stripped of their treasure in minutes. The grain was loaded into trucks and the trucks went directly to the grain elevators in surrounding towns. As the last rows were harvested, the machines pulled out of the fields and back onto the roads. Occasionally one of them stopped, grabbed a cup of coffee, mumbled a few words of uncomfortable sympathy when the widow and her family were present. They accepted expressions of gratitude but, clearly not used to the process, they often didn't even pause for that.

My sense of what was happening was not that the farmers simply wanted to be on their way to pick their own crops, but they were clearly embarrassed by the notion of being thanked for something that needed doing. We tried to talk with them on camera, to get some expression about how strong community is on the Plains, how important family is, how deeply tragedy runs in close-knit groups, how heritage, history, religion, and ethnicity requires this kind of cooperation, but there was none of that.

"Sorry, about your loss . . ."

"Anything else you need?"

"Thanks for the coffee and rolls, Bets."

"See you in church tomorrow, Father."

"When you finish that 80 of yours, can you swing over and finish up that little 20 of mine down by the creek, Ralph?"

One of the big grain trucks came rattling by, now empty. The driver approached the widow and her two children and handed her a handful of receipts from the elevator—over $100,000 worth of sales, enriched by the fact that this harvest, this year, there would be no overhead, no worries about storage and hauling. For this young, beautiful woman suddenly alone with her children, this year's harvest was done, in the span of a few hours, finished before noon. The truck driver nodded a brief acknowledgement to her expressions of gratitude and hurried to his truck, his hands in his overall pockets.

We left the scene totally bedazzled by what we had seen. Not just the fury of the accelerated harvest, not simply by the undirected (but obviously well rehearsed) ballet of the machines, but also by the unself-conscious dignity of the participants, all knowing that the same mechanism would go into operation for their families should something terrible happen to them. (But, please, there was not for a moment any indication that these people were doing this because they expected the same to be done for them; seriously, really, they were clearly doing what they were doing because it was the thing to do, the thing that needed doing!)

I couldn't help but say too to my old friends, Bud, Izzy, and Dan, how taken aback I was upon meeting the widow. I don't know why— perhaps because the farmer who died at the wheel of his tractor months earlier was in his early 50s, roughly my age. Perhaps because farmers on the Plains tend to be older than the average American. Whatever the reasons, I expected a weathered, older woman when we first went to the farmhouse for the interview I had been dreading for months.

My mistake. The widow in this case was a movie-star beautiful woman, young and alive, but with that soft, genuine beauty movie stars never manage to generate with makeup and lighting.

"It's probably a terrible thing to say," I said to my friends as we drove back across the state that evening, "but I had thoughts about a long, lonely, empty life for the widow before I met her. As young and pretty as she is, she'll find candidates for a new life-companion soon, I bet."

"And," Bud added with great insight, "there will never be a more protected young woman. With a community like that behind her, God help the man who doesn't treat her right. She's going to be all right."

And I hope she is.

Dogs

I suppose I should be embarrassed by how often I managed to sneak my family into camera range, especially Antonia. I visited her school, Centura Consolidated, a half dozen times; kids planting trees at school for Arbor Day, kids in the essay on goofy names people come up with for their children these days, and the story on school buses. There were a few scenes with Linda and Antonia at the house; eating one of my smoked hams for Christmas, pruning trees, fussing with the fireplace. But I couldn't engineer that sort of thing very often because Linda and Antonia never made it easy: they aren't as comfortable in front of the camera as I am and resisted every effort of mine to put them there.

Not so with the other beloved members of my family—my dogs.

I do love dogs. I have written elsewhere, only partly in jest, that I can't imagine for the life of me why anyone has a cat while there is still one surviving dog in this world. And that I find it eerily significant that "dog" spelled backwards is "god," while "kitty-cat" spelled backwards is "ticky-tack," sort of.

Okay, okay, we do have a house cat I have learned to respect, even love, formally named by Antonia "Love-Heart Love-Kitty Love-Angel" ("Hairball" for short). And we have a back porch cat, Homer, so named because, despite some really serious efforts on our part to get rid of him, he managed to find his way back here ("home") unerringly, over miles and miles of open country. And I respect—even admire—him for that.

And there's my shop kitty, Cindy Clawford, whom I sort of like too.

But not like I love my dogs.

And that's probably important too: *my* dogs. There are plenty of dogs I don't like. We did a Postcard, for example, on farm dogs. My intention was to show dogs hard at work being farm dogs; guarding farmyards, escorting children to the school bus stop, helping Mom pick up the mail from the box out by the road, checking on household security, that kind of thing. Unfortunately, that's not the way our story turned out.

I'm not sure if I was just flat-out wrong about farm dogs, or if we had a particularly bad day finding authentic farm dogs, or if it was just a bad day for dogs in general. But all we found in our 12-hour search of farms within 20 miles of my place were mean, ugly, back-biting, sneaky, snarly, unpleasant, unfriendly, unregenerate mutts. Or maybe they all just had it in for Izzy. But whatever the case, we had a day full of ugly dogs when we did that piece.

We almost got eaten alive by Johnny Fanta's dogs. Izzy shot footage of them from our open van door as we cruised through Johnny's yard; the dogs almost got into the van, which would have been pretty exciting for the four of us who were already in there, and then they bit our tires. They didn't just bark at them, or snap at them—they *bit* them.

Actually, I believe all dogs worthy of the noble title of "dog" should be (1) big, and (2) black, preferably (3) big and black. Johnny Fanta's dogs were not big and black, just little, mean, and ugly. Yappy little rat-dogs need another label of some kind. Not "dog." Not big, not black = not dog.

With some exceptions. Cornflake and Blaze, subjects of two of our Postcards, come to mind. Cornflake and Blaze were neither big nor black but boy, were they ever dogs. They're in canine heaven now. I'm not sure where that is. Some Bible thumpers around here say there isn't such a thing as dog heaven because only blessed humans as pious (and, I presume, obnoxious) as they enjoy the love of God, but I insist there is. Given any choice at all whether I want to be in a heaven where there are dogs or one where there are self-righteous prigs . . . well, that isn't much of a choice, now, is it?

The Undying Loyalty of Cornflake

The story about Cornflake left me so damned mad, as my pal Mick Maun says, my jaw was tight. I first saw the story in a human-interest column in the *Omaha World-Herald* by another old friend, Bob McMorris. Someone had contacted him and told him there was an abandoned dog hanging around an Arby's restaurant near the town of Elkhorn, just west of Omaha. Someone had dumped him out of a car there and the dog had been sitting faithfully waiting alongside the highway ever since, waiting for the miserable swine of a human being who had betrayed him so badly months before. While we're talking about Heaven, let's consider the sublime joy of hoping there's a hell for miserable wretches like that!

The dog sat there through a searing Nebraska summer, and then an arctic Nebraska winter. People pained by the dog's quiet vigil tried to feed him, with only modest success. They built him a little house where he could get out of the weather. They tried to capture him to give him medical care and perhaps a home, but without success. They named the dog "Cornflake"—for one of his few culinary preferences, as I recall.

I thought the plight of the dog would be a great opportunity to underscore the villainy of cruds who dump pets like this and to celebrate people who go out of their way to feed, house, and care for dogs who remain faithful in the face of faithlessness.

We made arrangements to visit the Arby's and interview some of the people involved in the effort to rescue Cornflake, but they warned us that we might have trouble bringing the story together because Cornflake had proven incredibly bashful when journalists had tried to see him. They said that our only chance would be shortly after dawn, or shortly after sunset.

Well, our schedule simply didn't allow that kind of flexibility. We could be there about nine in the morning, and we could stay until perhaps three in the afternoon. But if we didn't have footage of Cornflake by then, well, there just wouldn't be any footage of Cornflake. Bud promised us that he'd work on images, presuming we wouldn't have anything of the phantom dog himself.

The next day, in the Arby's parking lot, we met our friends—Cornflake's friends—and found that we had indeed missed him. He had passed through early that morning, grabbed some food, and disappeared into a cornfield behind his little house. Bud's strategy was to shoot my on-camera work in the cornfield, panning down to a few of the dog's tracks in the soft earth of the field. That would work. It had to. Those paw prints in soft loam were almost certainly going to be as close as we were going to get to the dog itself.

But then as we were shooting my on-camera lines, Izzy sputtered, "Over there! Is that him?!"

It was. Cornflake was watching us at work. He was a good 100 yards away, maybe more, but Izzy squeezed the most out of his camera and got us a few moments of doggie footage, enough to get us through the story. Perhaps.

We finished our interviews, did my stand-ups, interviewed the manager of the Arby's, and sat down for a quick lunch before we had to move on to the next story, many hours down the road. As we sat in a booth, eating a sandwich, Izzy suddenly sputtered yet once again, "My God! There he is. Walking right through the #$@%&*& parking lot!!" And sure enough, here came the dog, trotting along through the parking lot in full daylight, something everyone before and since assured us he had never done before. We had hit the impossible odds.

Izzy scrambled to the door, and eased his way out. The dog stopped in his tracks, eyed Izzy uneasily. Izzy edged inch by inch toward the van and his camera. The dog backed up, glancing uneasily toward the safety of the cornfield.

Then Izzy did something that had us still in the restaurant screaming vicious curses in his direction: he straightened up, walked briskly and directly toward the van, opened the door, hauled out his camera, slamming the door behind him, and walked from the van in the general direction of the dog.

I should have known. One of the requirements we have for Izzy when he is here is that he work with our dogs. He has an uncanny ability to deal with canines. Linda explains that we are having trouble keeping the dogs from going out the gate, from jumping up on visitors, from barking at cars, from chasing the cats, or whatever the case may be. And in moments Iz does whatever it takes to educate the respective dog. He just seems to know what he needs to do. Dogs seem to understand what Izzy is saying, and respond. In moments, the dog is cured of his evil spirits. It's amazing.

So, I should have known that Izzy was not being stupid, or difficult, which God knows, he is perfectly capable of being when he wants to be. Something had told Izzy that this dog was an expert at reading guile, subterfuge, and threat, and understandably feared it. As Izzy told us later, he noticed that while he was sneaking out to the van to get his camera, the dog carefully watching his every move, other people were moving around the restaurant walking, running, driving, getting in and out of vehicles, without the dog paying them the slightest attention. Izzy therefore deduced—correctly—that if he simply went about his business, the dog would no longer be suspicious.

And that's precisely what happened: Cornflake immediately lost interest in Izzy, resuming his search for scraps in the restaurant parking lot. Izzy took out his camera, set it up, and shot abundant footage of our elusive Postcard star, the dog topping the event off by strolling within feet of the camera while Izzy was shooting. It was a superb moment, a fine Postcard.

Sadly, hours before the piece was to air, I got a call from Elkhorn that the dog had been run over and killed the night before. Damn. The dog died under a car's tires, still waiting for his miserable, traitorous master. Maybe if there is a heaven, only dogs are there.

Charles Kuralt closed Cornflake's Postcard with a notice of his passing—as was always the case with Charles Kuralt, with genuine compassion and concern. The moral was all the stronger, perhaps, for Cornflake's death: given a choice, I'll take dogs every time.

Working Dogs

Blaze was another story I had to work at for a long time before things finally came together for a shooting. It was, I think, in the early 1970s or late 1960s that I was in Europe for a conference on ethnological foodways studies. I spent a few days before the conference on a farm near Leads, England, with old friend Jay Anderson, then of Penn State in Hershey, now of Utah State University in Logan.

I awoke one morning to hear the frantic barking of a dog somewhere near our farmhouse. I looked out the window and saw a beautiful collie working some sheep in a neighboring field. Some of the sheep were very thin and light-colored; others were very large and dark. I don't know a lot about sheep but I figured out fairly quickly that it must be the season for shearing. The light, skinny sheep had already lost their bulky outer fleece and the larger, dirtier ones were awaiting their moment under the shears.

I got dressed and hurried downstairs where Jay, his wife, and children were already at the breakfast table. I told them what I had seen and suggested that we hurry over to the neighbor's farm and see if we could watch some sheep shearing. We did, and sure enough, there was an old gentleman hard at work with hand shears, snip-snip-snipping away.

Well, he was an interesting gent. He was the first from whom I heard what I later learned is an ancient jibe: I asked him how old he was and he said 87; I asked him how long he'd been farming and he said 87 years. I asked him what he had done those first few years, since he was only a babe in arms, and he replied, "Milked and spread manure."

He demonstrated and explained how he cut fleece, tied them, treated sheep for cuts and parasites, and trimmed their hooves. It was a wonderful seminar in the traditions of ovine husbandry.

Then we heard the terrible wailing of Jay's children, screaming bloody murder. "Oh my God," our host growled. "That damned dog!"

I took off running toward the sound of the screams, presuming that the murderous collie was disemboweling the children. Behind the barn I found the children whining and howling as the dog joyfully herded them from one end of the small livestock pen to the other. The collie, it turned out, was so enthusiastic about this day of doing what he was bred to do—herd—that he just couldn't bring himself to waste idle time and nominal "livestock" by standing around. So he was herding children. Seemed harmless enough to him. As I think on it, seems harmless enough to me.

The farmer scolded the dog firmly, however, and the dog seemed to understand the order if not the logic behind it. I could see in his eyes that he simply couldn't understand why he couldn't just herd the children for a little while at least. What harm could it do?! But no . . .

The children, still sobbing, joined us at the front of the barn, but soon we heard the dog barking again, and here he came, rejoicing in a new activity—herding grasshoppers. No kidding, that dog was busily herding a swarm of grasshoppers from one end of the farm to the other and back. Barking gleefully, doing his job.

I was ready, therefore, when a couple days later, Jay, his family, and I were in a public park, watching an exhibit of sheep dogs at work. If you haven't seen it yourself, you need to. The dogs do the herding, you know, with their eyes. They stare. I don't know if they "read" the sheep, or the sheep "read" them, but they control the sheep with their eyes. And like the farmer's collie, they are never quite as happy as they are when they are doing what they are supposed to do—herd. And there's nothing I love more than watching dogs do what they are supposed to do.

Small wonder then that one year when Linda, Antonia, and I were leaving the parking lot of the Nebraska State Fair in Lincoln, passing by an open-arena building, and we heard an announcer talking about the upcoming event—working dogs—that I pulled my family away from their determined path toward the midway and the quilting exhibits toward the working dog exhibition. I think they wound up fairly well amazed by the skills of the dogs and their handlers by the time we left.

As we exited, I stepped over to the announcer's booth, handed up one of my business cards, and explained that I sure would like to talk with someone using working dogs in the area of Dannebrog. The man behind the microphone assured me he would pass along my card, and apparently he did, because it wasn't long before I heard from Shane Bader, a cattle producer living not far from my own place. He uses, he explained, working dogs to handle his cattle. "A dog is worth two men," he explained. "At least."

Blaze

He said he would be making a major cattle drive soon, moving 100 head of cattle or so cross-country and down county roads to new pasturage on some cornstalks. The men would be on horseback, and he would be using his dog Blaze, and maybe one of her pups to move the herd. To me it sounded like a perfect set-up for a Postcard.

The day started off cold and snowy but turned beautiful and sunny. The countryside near Wolbach, Nebraska, is hilly and rugged. Tough riding and hard herding, but great scenics for the camera.

And Blaze worked up to promise. She ran and ran and ran. Nothing escaped her attention. If there was a problem for us with the television camera, it was that she was *all* business. She had no time for television, no time to stop, no time to turn an eye toward the camera. She cut herself on a barbed wire fence and Shane had to dress her wound, but even then she whined and cried, not out of pain but eager to be on her way, utterly without patience for the minor inconvenience of the 4-inch gash on her foreleg.

The best shot of the day never made it, as I recall, into the piece as aired. Izzy, ever the inventive and artistic cinematographer, lay down in the back of a pickup truck rolling at a good speed in front of the herd. He held his camera almost at ground level and captured the image of Blaze running straight ahead at him, right in front of the grinding hooves of more than 100 cattle, each 50 to 100 times his size. (And—this is the secret, of course—each with 1/100 his intelligence and determination!)

Probably the funniest event of the day has never found its way to print or broadcast either. In fact, Bud is going to kill me when he reads this because one of the cardinal, tacit rules of broadcast journalism is that what happens on the road, stays on the road. Well, I'm not really a journalist.

The herd we were moving was made up of cows, their heifer calves, and some steers—young, castrated bulls. And one bull. The situation was that a neighbor's bull had found his way across a couple barbed wire fences into the Baders' herd. So, the neighbor was there on his horse, planning to cut his bull out of the herd and move it back across the fence to his own property as the herd passed close. It would be a fairly easy, fairly comfortable transaction, requiring no particular, special effort on anyone's part.

The neighbor moved his bull from the herd and off in another direction while we moved on; Izzy, Dan, Bud, and I in a pickup truck, shooting from hillside to hillside as Blaze worked his heart out. At one point Bud and Izzy got out of the truck bed to shoot from ground level as the herd moved by, but Bud expressed some concern because a couple bulls were eyeing him menacingly. Whoops. There weren't supposed to be any bulls in the herd now that the neighbor's was gone. But Bud assured us, bulls there were.

Shane Bader's wife hurried over to tell Shane that a couple bulls had been spotted in the herd. The men on horseback stopped the herd to take account of what the heck was going on. Shane rode over and asked if we had noticed any identifying marks on the bulls Bud had seen. I hadn't even seen the bulls so I couldn't be much help. Bud pointed out the bulls that had him worried.

Shane looked at Bud with a peculiar look on his face. Shane is a tough, no-nonsense cattleman, but like the cowboys of the Classic Era, he is also a gentleman, not about to offend a guest.

Well, Bud was pointing at every animal with horns—a New Yorker's idea, I guess, of what separates the cows and steers from the bulls. I started to explain that horns aren't the difference between bulls and steers. Then it occurred to me that I had never been very successful in the past with such lessons in rural living to Bud and the Scud Bubbas, so I shrugged my shoulders, smiled and winked in the direction of Shane and his drovers. And we all moved along down the trail. To this day, whenever I see Shane Bader or one of the men who were with us that day, there is certain to be a comment about how they wonder what the difference is between cows and bulls back East!

The sad part of the story of Blaze, the inevitable part of the story of Blaze, is that I heard not long afterward that Blaze died "in the saddle," as it were. She was kicked hard by an angry beeve and died from internal injuries. Shane told me when we were shooting our story that he does everything he can not to get any more fond of his working dogs than he does of his cowboy buddies because it's a hard life and the consequences come all too soon, all too often.

"Just can't make that kind of investment in your livestock or dogs," he said. It was not a statement of indifference or cruelty but one of self-preservation. I had seen enough of Blaze to know that's what she would have felt too. No time for a gashed leg during work. No time to mourn the death of a good worker.

Moreover, I feel that way about a lot of deaths. When the sainted Charles Kuralt died, I was shattered. He was like a guardian angel to me. But I decided not to mourn. Instead, I have devoted whatever energy I would have spent feeling sorry for him, or more honestly for me, being grateful that he graced our lives as long as he did—all our lives—and that for 30-plus years I had the incredible gift of calling him a friend.

I consider one of the major disadvantages of being a human that our dogs tend to die before we do. And that's a kind of pain I don't want to face very often in my life. That's one of the reasons I have two black labs. When my beautiful boy Black Jack died a few years ago, I swore that I would never again be left in my life without a backup black dog, and I meant it. I'm too old to spend any more of my days than necessary without a big, black dog, and I won't. If I had my way, no one would ever spend a day without a big, black dog.

Unless it's a little, brown dog like Cornflake or Blaze. They were dogs. Real dogs.

Native American Issues

One of the many reasons I was delighted when Charles gave me the opportunity to be a part of CBS's "Sunday Morning," was that I was at a moment in the middle of a painful and dramatic struggle that seemed to me to be prime material for a serious Postcard from Nebraska.

The Nebraska State Historical Society doesn't seem like the sort of agency that would arouse much in the way of passion. And it shouldn't. History is history, despite the quotation ascribed to Harry Truman that ". . . the trouble with history is that it's just one damned thing after another." A state historical society deals with the pride of a region's people after all. How, starting with that kind of goodwill and support, could a state historical society possibly be controversial?

Well, in 1987 the executive board, director, and some staff of the Nebraska State Historical Society were busily digging themselves into a hole just as fast and deep as they could, seemingly ignorant of any possibility of resistance from the membership or general citizenry.

There were suspicions and rumors of other misappropriations and scandals. As the grumbles grew louder within and without the society, the chief official simply tightened his already choking, dictatorial grasp. This was with the approval and even help of a board that was supposed to be supervising him, but was instead abetting in the destruction of a grand institution many of us loved and needed for our life's work.

A group within the society's membership finally decided it was time our voices be heard, and we decided to nominate some candidates for election to the board at the next annual meeting. Now, annual meetings of the society were always utterly predictable, utterly controlled by the director and his handpicked board, so they did not take this challenge lightly. In fact, they abrogated the election, denying members the right to vote, refusing an accounting of the votes, simply commandeering the election process. I was one of those candidates, almost certainly elected to the board but denied a seat.

Since a substantial proportion of the society's support was provided by the state, we dissidents next turned to the legislature for relief, and found substantial support. As the struggle got nastier and nastier, the society czar's position grew ever shakier. And he finally resigned—taking the reins of the society's foundation, thereby putting himself in a position for continued convolutions and convulsions that are still being uncovered and corrected.

But the problem was at least diminished in terms of the leadership of the society. We thought. A new director (a professional historian) was appointed by the board, which was now chastened and cautioned by the new attention from state officials. The new director was young, dynamic, and promising. We thought.

Perhaps because we had just gone through such bloodletting, perhaps because, as Nebraskans, we tend to be too trustful, perhaps because this guy was drenched with charm, perhaps because we again couldn't imagine anyone being stupid enough to throw away the new, fat treasure of goodwill enjoyed by the society, we trusted him to do things right.

We were disappointed, to say the least. Those in favor on the society's staff soared in power and reward, and those who resisted such things as signing fraudulent reports on allocations of federal funding were sent into limbo.

Pawnee Bones

The final straw—not exactly a subtle one—came when a group of Pawnee elders, spiritual leaders, and political figures came to the society to petition for the repatriation of their dead, some of whom had lain on society shelves in cardboard boxes for many decades. The Pawnee request was submitted humbly and quietly. Their people had buried their dead with the intention that they rest in peace forever. But the graves had been excavated, sometimes by scholars, sometimes by amateur diggers.

In some cases the human remains and the cultural artifacts had been examined, studied, documented, and in some cases even put on exhibit, contrary to tribal belief (and for that matter, human decency). The Pawnee simply wanted to make arrangements to reclaim their dead and rebury them.

One could argue, of course, that such remains are historical artifacts, scientific specimens. Unfortunately, the people who were most vocal in such assertions made no such claims about the remains of white pioneers, homesteaders, Oregon Trailers, and soldiers, who, when exhumed for whatever reason, are inevitably and speedily reburied, with honors and dignity. The lesson was unavoidable: white folks are human beings; Indians are specimens and artifacts.

As a member of the Historical Society's board, I listened carefully. I went into this issue totally objectively. I had made no prior conclusions. These were invaluable, irreplaceable cultural artifacts we were talking about destroying, in effect. As a member of the University of Nebraska's Anthropology Department, I understood what the loss would be for scholars. As a friend of the Native American community (but not, at that point, of the Pawnee), I knew the intensity of their feelings about this violation of their dead, but that of all people, no one had more to learn from the archeologists' research than the Pawnee themselves.

I saw there was considerable latitude within the Indians' positions: some insisted on an immediate return of the remains and absolutely no further research on materials held by the society then, or ever held by the society in the future. Others urged a middle course of brief, prompt study, but then a return of the remains to Mother Earth.

I listened not only to the Pawnee but also to my Omaha relatives, especially my brother, Alfred Gilpin Jr. I listened to people I respect deeply, like Louis LaRose of the Winnebago and Calvin Iron Shell, a Lakota. They expressed their concerns and hopes with dignity, eloquence, reason, and sincerity.

And in astonishment and shame I listened to the director of the society and several colluding members of the board of directors, sneering their contempt for the Pawnee delegation. The director referred to the Pawnee as "outsiders." (They had been forcibly expelled from their Nebraska lands a century before.)

Meetings were scheduled, the Pawnee traveled long distances to discuss the situation, only to find that the society officials stood them up—they had more important things to do. Other board members, often historians who should have known better, ignored clear society policy, professional ethics, common courtesy, and good sense.

Finally, I resigned from the Historical Society Board and joined forces with the Pawnee and the Native American Rights Fund. It was clear to me that the Indians were not only right, but also that their tormentors were at best stupid, at worst evil.

It was at just about this point that I began sending my Postcards from Nebraska via "Sunday Morning." I wrestled with the problem of objectivity, and conflict of interest, but I am not a journalist or a reporter. I am an essayist. A "postcard" is a personal expression, a note from one's observations and emotions. And boy, was that the case with this situation!

So, my first Native American Postcard was brief coverage of the Pawnee bones issue, and it turned out to be one of the few hard news stories I did during my 10 years of writing essays. The response was immense. I got a few letters from scholars, scientists, and bigots protesting my softheartedness (and softheadedness), but far more from those who were astonished and appalled at the society's official insensitivity.

I like to think that Postcard contributed to the eventual collapse of Historical Society resistance to the Pawnee petitions, a turnover in board membership reflecting a new morality (a later, very influential and positive chair of the board was Charles Trimble, a Lakota!), and the appointment of Larry Sommer, a man with the support and respect of the Native American community.

On two occasions since those wars, I have been asked by the Pawnee to serve as "pallbearer" at repatriation ceremonies; I have now assisted in the retrieval and reburial of almost 1000 Pawnee in Nebraska—in Pawnee soil. I couldn't be more proud.

Vision Gets the Green Light

Producer Bud Lamoreaux wisely detected the wider significance of the story's reception across the nation, noting that there is almost no coverage of news within the Native American community. He urged me to watch for other stories that would showcase tribal culture and activity, and I was more than happy to do just that. In fact, of all topics we covered in our 10 years and almost 180 Postcards, Native American stories were our most common topic, serving as the subject of at least 10 full essays with mention or inclusion in another dozen. Frankly, if I could, I'd like to be able to send a Postcard from Native America once a month.

I'm not sure my psyche could handle the strain however. The story of Native Americans can be pretty discouraging. For example, one of my Postcards was a peek at the past, but very close to my own heart and my own land at Dannebrog; the recognition of the historic government residence school at Genoa, Nebraska, within sight of where we eventually buried the remains of the violated Pawnee.

The schools were not nice places; an explicit agenda was "Kill the Indian to save the man." For those of us who feel it was civilization's loss to kill the Indian, schools like Genoa are not pleasant places to be. I'll have to admit, I was surprised as I talked with old alums (the school closed, after all, in 1934) to find that some were actually grateful for their years there. They told me that conditions on the reservations were so grim, there was a good chance they would have died or become seriously ill. And they certainly wouldn't have gotten a decent education(!) if it hadn't been for the Genoa school and the government program.

My concern, I guess, is selfish: I would prefer that the power of Native American culture be strong and available for those of us who need it rather than erased, whatever the motivation or immediate advantage. I recall hearing my old Omaha friends and relatives talking about their years at the school (although there aren't many left now who remember) and their proud refusal to let the Indian within them die.

Especially vivid is an occasion when I was standing outside the old Lincoln, Nebraska, municipal swimming pool bathhouse awaiting the start of a traditional Omaha handgame (a kind of competitive button-button-who has the button), chatting with Oliver Saunsoci Sr., Clyde and Frank Sheridan, Charles Stabler—some of the old-timers.

A small boy ran by and we all laughed because he was such a mess: he was wearing khaki pants and had stuffed a chocolate bar in his pocket. It had, of course, melted, and now his pants sported a huge, greasy stain. "Looks like us when we were at the Genoa School," one of my friends laughed.

I expressed my curiosity and they explained that one of the ways the school tried to remove their Indianness was to feed them white man's food. But they thwarted the intent by bringing a small iron pan from home, and occasionally filching small bits of fat from the supper table (thus staining their pockets and pants), running to the nearby Loup River woods, stealing a couple ears of field corn along the way. They'd build a fire down by the river and with the fat, parch the corn, thus producing Indian food—which kept them Indian.

I laughed too, but the thought of my people trying to crush the proud heritage out of these people I had come to love filled me with shame and regret. That evening I ate my Indian food at the feast, which always follows the handgame, with special relish, hoping that my Omaha friends were right about "culture by ingestion!"

The most shattering narrative of our day at the Genoa School came not from an Indian but from a Genoa resident, and it never made the camera or the screen. A woman told me she had grown up in Genoa, near the school, and so she'd seen the school in operation during the early years of her own life, even though she wasn't a student there.

I asked her what she felt about the school when she was young, or even now that she was older and the school was closed. She hesitated and her eyes misted over. She said, almost sobbing, that even as a child she had looked at the school and its work with horror. She said she could still hear, see, and feel the agony of the Indian families bringing their beloved children to the school, leaving them there for perhaps years before they would see them again.

Imagine that pain! Indian families are very close, and children are special treasures. Leaving them by requirement of law would be one thing, but the torture of wrestling with the reality that the imminent long absence at such great distance might be the only thing between your child and death . . . Not a pretty situation.

The woman illustrated the pain she had witnessed by telling me a story of a Lakota family that had brought their young son to Genoa, a trip that took many days back then, over bad roads, even with their ancient automobile. She said that the family's car broke down just a few hundred yards from the school, so it was pulled to the school's shops for repair while the boy went through the procedures of registration. The problem, it turned out, was minor—a broken fan belt—so the car was quickly repaired.

The mother wailed piteously as their car drove off, leaving her son behind, in this strange place, for so long a time, 300 miles away from Lakota land, a million miles away from Lakota culture. Her cries, the woman told me, could be heard until the auto was well out of the town's boundaries.

I was shaken by the image, but the hard part of the story was yet to come. After the car had gone, the boy escaped his captors at the school at the very first opportunity, just long enough to get to the blacksmith shop where his family's car was repaired, where he retrieved the broken fan belt. It was the only thing he had of his poor, unpropertied family. The only token, the only possession he would be able to clutch for at least a year, perhaps more, before he saw them again. A broken fan belt!

When the woman finished telling me her story, she was in tears. And she wasn't alone.

Omaha Color and Culture

Among my own Omaha people, we did three stories. The first was on the annual powwow, with its wonderful color and flash and music. I only wish we could have shared with our viewers the smell of fresh fry bread and the taste of corn soup!

That was easy enough: it fit in with the stories we did on ethnic and historical festivals in other Nebraska towns. As part of the story, I did an interview with my Omaha brother, Alfred "Buddy" Gilpin, a man from whom I learned so much about life. It was one of the last times I saw him alive, and the taped moments of that interview are among my personal treasures.

Later, in a hall named for Buddy, we did a story on the traditional Omaha handgame I mentioned before. It's a game of ritualized pony stealing, much as Monopoly is a game of ritualized capitalism. Again, the music, dance, and laughter of the Omaha people at the game made it an easy story to record and send to America.

I am a strong believer in context, especially cultural context. It is one thing to enjoy a bit of native art, or food, or song, but it is quite another, much more satisfying and instructive experience to take in those things where they are at home; in a village, home, social gathering, or foreign land. On one occasion we wrenched that notion about as hard as it can be wrenched.

I sat at the Omaha tribal drum trying to learn Omaha songs for almost a decade. I didn't learn many songs but I did learn that the Omaha repertoire is so vast that it would take a lifetime and serious work to learn it. And I learned that the aesthetic requirements of singing at that drum, even passably well, are well beyond my meager talents. So, as you can imagine, I tend to bristle when anyone suggests that Omaha music is anything less demanding, powerful, or glorious than western art music.

I was therefore fascinated when I learned that a symphony had been written combining traditional Omaha music with symphonic orchestration. Not just a melody line or mood, mind you, but an Omaha drum played by practitioners of Omaha music within the body of a traditional symphonic orchestra. The setting was powerful. For one thing, the concert was in the City of Omaha's glorious Orpheum Theatre, about as beautiful a building as ever built. For another, I was a performer, a storyteller for the evening.

The context of any symphony is dramatic, as is the context of any Omaha musical performance. The symphonic music was fine, quite good. But my God, when the great drum of the Omaha began to throb in the midst of that conventional musical performance setting, the effect was electric. The audience was not just impressed; it was shaken. The performance ended with a standing ovation. It was spectacular.

As was my tuxedo.

On another occasion we returned to the Omaha reservation at Macy, an hour north of Omaha, Nebraska, to tape a story about an art project by a talented teacher from the University of Nebraska at Kearney, Al Kraning. Al was helping a local Macy art teacher work with her students by teaching them film animation. He'd sent me

69

a copy of a tape with some of the animation and asked me to look at it.

Well, I never look at story ideas people send me on videotape. I just don't have time for it. I can read a quick introduction to an idea in a matter of seconds, and pretty much tell if it has potential or not. To sit down and watch a videotape—especially amateur videotape—eats up a good half-hour or more, and is rarely of use. So, I resisted. But my wife Linda was taking art classes at this school, and she took a class from this teacher, and so . . . growl, grump . . . I'd look at the damned tape.

I was stunned. The animation was interesting (if not great) but more than that, it was ethnological. These were not cartoons about Indian culture by children. They were fundamentally Native American films. Not only was the content Omaha, the film itself was Omaha.

For example, one brief cartoon animation was of a buffalo hunt. The boy who did the film based his cartoon animation on what he'd been told about buffalo hunts by his elders; thus, this was not just a cartoon but a historical document. The short film showed a young Omaha crawling through tall grass and bushes close to a small herd of bison, raising up to shoot his bow, firing an arrow—and missing. The buffalo ran off, leaving the boy to retrieve his arrow and try again later.

Does that sound like a white man's film to you? It sure doesn't to me! In a white man's film, the Indian would have killed his prey. But that's not the way Omaha thought works. Omahas live in a passive world where things happen. The white man lives in a world where he makes things happen. A white man tells his children they can grow up to be whatever they want to be: an obvious absurdity. An Omaha misses a bus and says, "The bus left without me." Which is, in a way, true.

It's probably a historical view. Either the buffalo came or they didn't. The corn grew or it didn't. You lived or you died. They learned to live in a world like that, and to understand it. And in this case, to capture it on film and show it to us. It made a great Postcard from Nebraska ("Nebraska" being the Omaha word for the Platte River, incidentally).

From Dust to Dust

We sent a Postcard from the Ponca, very close cousins of the Omaha, when that tribe returned to Nebraska and reestablished their tribe on ancient Ponca land. With the help, by the way, of their Omaha kin. Just to the north of the Omaha reservation in Thurston

County, Nebraska, sharing a long border with it, is the Winnebago reservation.

The United States government, in its historical savagery, traded the Winnebagos out of some of their native ground in Wisconsin, giving them instead some land in South Dakota. It's bad enough that South Dakota sure as hell isn't Wisconsin, but there was also the little technicality that the land had already been traded to the fierce Lakota. That sort of trade was common to the period in which the Lakota were given some land they already had for land the white guys wanted! The Winnebago, upon arrival in their new, private hell, were driven off, down the Missouri River, winding up on land ceded to them by the Omaha from their lands.

Louis LaRose, curator of the Winnebago bison herd, spent the day with us, telling us about the power of his brethren, the buffalo. It was a beautiful day, they were beautiful animals, and Louie was a great interview. There were, however, two problems with the day's shoot.

First, I wasn't able to cover the story I really wanted to tell. Louie had told me his secret plans for the bison land, an idea that had knocked me out of my seat the first time I heard it a few months earlier. Louis faced some enormous hurdles in his love for his buffalo and his intention to build a large, permanent herd on the Missouri River bluffs of his people's reservation. Within his tribe, there were those who saw the bison herd only as a short-term, meat-producing project. They wondered aloud how long Louis intended to continue it.

Forever, he explained to us.

But that would require money, continuing support, apart from the tribe, apart from the government, apart from charity, apart from political and economic shifts. And he had a plan: he was going to declare his buffalo range a burial ground. He got the idea when the Pawnee were struggling to find a place to bury their reclaimed dead. He would make burial sites available on his buffalo range for any tribe that needed ground for its old dead. And he would make ground available for others, Indians and non-Indians both, who really believed in the notion that they came from dust and should return to dust.

"If you are buried on my place," Louis laughed, "I'll guarantee you that by morning some big old buffalo bull will be rolling on top of you, dusting himself on the loose dirt of your grave."

Louis told that to me during a telephone conversation and I almost fell apart. I ran to the house tears running down my face to tell Linda that at last I had an answer to my dread of the white man's way of death—embalming, encapsulating, sealing, vaulting, cement, stone, eternity . . . apart from the earth and soil to which we are to return.

"I'll wrap you up in a Pendleton blanket," Louis promised me, ". . . maybe put some boards over you, and you will be asleep in our Mother Earth." God, what a relief that idea was for me.

But when we shot our Postcard with Louis, he wasn't ready to make his plan public. So we didn't mention it, the really big story unspoken.

And yet it would have been appropriate, because I was literally at the verge of dying. We taped the buffalo Postcard with Louis on Tuesday, April 16. Hours before, April 15, in a motel in South Sioux City, Nebraska, I'd had a heart attack. I was sick, and I knew it. I was dizzy, nauseated, shaky, unsteady on my feet. I was grayish, and my vision blurred. I got through the day, but just barely. I didn't want to be a sissy. I didn't want to be the boy who cried "Wolf." And I was almost the boy who died precisely where he wanted to be buried.

That would have been a nice touch.

Remembrance and Heritage

We did two essays about Lakota issues. On a bitter cold day in 1990 we flew to Valentine, Nebraska, rented a car, and drove into South Dakota and onto the Pine Ridge Reservation of the Oglala Sioux to do an essay on the anniversary of the Massacre at Wounded Knee. It was a painful story, in the bitter, bitter cold. But it wasn't as cold as it had been 100 years earlier when the old, sick, and exhausted people of Big Foot's band died under a hailstorm of exploding shells from the 7th Iowa's automatic Hotchkiss guns.

It was the only story, I think, that we did completely outside the state of Nebraska and on a subject not really a Nebraska story. But I thought it was important to remind America of that terrible event. I think we should remember and observe as a national holiday Wounded Knee. Every year. Perhaps when we celebrate our glories, we should also remember our shames.

In Alliance, Nebraska, we shot a story about a summer camp for kids. Not just another summer camp, not just more kids, but Lakota children from the western Nebraska area, attending a summer camp under the guidance of Connie and Gary Stairs. The Stairses spent their week with them teaching Lakota culture, ways, food, song, story, art, and religion.

The only thing that bothered me about the story was that I wished I'd been able to attend a camp like that when I was young. Or now, for that matter. As I have argued for years, it seems a shame that the beauty and power of Native American ways are so often restricted in one way or another to Native Americans. If only our pioneer ancestors would've had the good sense to do more listening and less ordering around!

Of all the Postcards I've sent America, I am most proud of those I sent from Native American sources. My contacts with Indians have been so important to me. I have always wanted to shout to others that Native American culture is important, not just as a curiosity, but as guidelines for life. Our life. Even us white guys. My intent has been to bring new respect and honor to Native Americans by celebrating their ways, and new wisdom and hope to non-Native Americans in the same way. Conversations and letters from "Sunday Morning" viewers suggest that to some small degree, I was successful in that endeavor.

Bringing the Long Gone to the Screen

It was also in these stories I leaned most heavily on my old friend, colleague, and student John Carter, photo curator at the Nebraska State Historical Society. One of the things I learned very early in my television career, such as it is, is that it is one thing to cover history in the making, quite another to cover history past. And it was a lesson I had to pass along more often than was comfortable for me.

I have always been appreciative when folks have sent me ideas for Postcard stories—we've wound up using a lot of them. But after a while even I, with my utter ignorance of television experience, could spot an unfeasible story when it came along. I think especially of a couple suggestions about the ever-popular, legendary Jesse James.

One suggestion was from an amateur enthusiast who pounded on me postally with the idea of covering the exhumation of what were allegedly the remains of Jesse near his old home in Kearny, Missouri. Well, for one thing, I have put a lot of my energy into resisting the idea of digging up dead people for the amusement of the living (I am thinking of the Pawnee issue!) but in this case I also had some discomfort imagining a "Sunday Morning" audience being invited to witness, over their morning coffee and bagels, the digging up of an old—very old—corpse.

A second suggestion for a Jesse James story was more typical; a note from a man who said he could show me the exact place on a nearby farm pasture where there had once been a hotel where Jesse James had reportedly slept.

Hmmm. As Bud put it so well, "Give me Jesse James and we'll do the story." The point is, there's only so much you can do with nonexistent historical information. As Bud also says, "Rog, this isn't radio. This is *teevee*. You know, Rog—radio with pictures!"

What did save us repeatedly over our decade of producing Postcards from Nebraska however, were the historical photographs supplied us by John Carter. Historical images were always the easiest part of our job . . . just call John, tell him what we need, and show up roughly on time to shoot. To be sure, a lot of credit is due the remarkable collection John works with, but a lot of whatever success we've enjoyed did come as a result of John's generous and cheerful help. God bless him.

Dannebrog

I brought CBS to Dannebrog with the same intentions I had with Native American stories: to share with others the details of a wonderful subculture I found so attractive myself. I came to this town originally totally by accident, but I stayed by choice and eventually moved here with determination. I love my little 60-acre piece of ground down along the Middle Loup River—I feel it is magic and that I am here by virtue of a grander design. I love America's rural countryside and small towns, and I've taken a little flak for that.

Once, before I started sending Postcards via "Sunday Morning," when I came here to use my cabin by the river as a retreat, I was exulting about the wonderfulness of small-town life and someone in town (I don't recall who) called me to task for it. "Of course you think life in this little burg is terrific," she said. "You come here for a day or two at a time, use it for a vacation spot, a recreation area. I think you'd have a different view of things if you had to live here."

To some degree she was right. In our 15 years of residence here we have discovered the less attractive side of small town life: small minds, religious zealots who would throw away the Constitution in a moment if it meant they could impose their shallow faith on the rest of us, haters and thieves, parasites and prigs, hypocrites and gossips. But when the woman scolded me years ago, I answered that perhaps that was my job, reminding people who have to live in towns like this, who have seen so much of the ugliness of small towns and farm life that they have forgotten the good side, the pretty side. I've been here a while now; so, it's my turn to try to remember that too.

Life in Dannebrog is not idyllic. It's real. I haven't made much of an issue on television of the unpleasantness because I feel the conventional media make enough of a fuss about that. It's true: I've been a good-news sort of reporter, with few exceptions. One of the most common questions I am asked (besides, "Do you really live in Dannebrog?" and, "What is Charles Kuralt

. . ." or now, ". . . Osgood really like?"), is, "Have your Postcards changed Dannebrog?"

And the answer is . . . uh, yes and no. On one hand, Dannebrog's principal industry has changed from servicing local farmers in the neighborhood with fuel, fertilizer, groceries, and news (at Eric's Tavern), to tourism. Now there are three gift shops in town, three tourist information stations, postcard racks, film, and souvenirs. We have two posh bed-and-breakfasts. (Even though one local snorted when the idea was first floated in town, "It'll never go over. Not everyone likes to eat breakfast in bed!")

I'm told that a huge map of the United States in the Denver airport shows two towns in Nebraska: Omaha—and Dannebrog. Thousands of cars leave Interstate-80, 25 miles south of Dannebrog, to come through this town every year, from all parts of the world, to see if it is really as advertised, if it is indeed what they have seen on "Sunday Morning." Generally of course it is.

Except maybe more so: many stories shot from hundreds of different angles have made the little town seem much larger than it really is, visitors find. Our main street is less than a full block long, and then almost completely on one side of the street. Doesn't take long to make the complete tour! There are 324 residents in Dannebrog, less than you would normally find on one side of a street for one block in Manhattan on a normal day, at a slow hour.

Remarkably, all that attention hasn't done much to change the people of the town, however. A member of the Dannebrog Booster Club recently noted that that group had done wonders in bringing attention to the town, because 10 years ago hardly anyone knew about Dannebrog and today it is famous all across America! His impression, it seems, is that the mural on the side of the American Legion building, the flower bed in front of Harriett's Danish Cafe, and the new paint job on the water tower brought all these tourists to town.

This particular "booster" is representative, I suspect, in that even he hasn't noticed CBS's repeated presence in his town over the same decade. He doesn't watch "Sunday Morning," probably wonders what channel it is on. He is, in short, oblivious of the larger picture. And that's why I live here. The big picture isn't all that interesting or important.

Dannebrog is doing well. There is a boom in home construction and property values are soaring; 10 years ago abandoned houses stood everywhere and you could buy a nice place for less than $10,000, a castle for $35,000. Now relatively ordinary houses sell for $60,000. The Boosters have launched a flurry of features even a big, fancy town would envy; a hike-and-bike trail, park renovation, razing of abandoned properties, and cleanups of junked vehicles and buildings.

Plenty of Character(s)

The people of the town have changed somewhat, not so much a matter of being star-struck or wealthy but by way of attrition. A lot of the interesting, grand old characters of the town, people I moved here to enjoy, have gone. Rod Hat died just before we came out, and Bruce Davis not long ago. Dave Ratliff breezed in and breezed back out. Bumps Nielsen is gone. Gaylord Obermiller and Lyle Fries moved away. We don't see much of Dee Steffenhagen anymore.

But there are still plenty of authentics to leaven the loaf. Dan, Bondo, Don, Al, Mel, Eric, Harriett, LaVon—and they make life here lively and interesting. I have always been surprised how quickly the town became utterly oblivious to a camera crew from a national network working in its streets. The tourists sometimes gather around to watch a Postcard in the making, but the citizens of Dannebrog rarely pay any attention at all to Izzy, Dan, and Bud behind a camera, me walking across Main Street toward them, talking into the lens. We and our work have become as much a usual part of this small town's life as Phil in the post office, Irma in the bank, or Marna at the flower shop. I like that. I think it makes our Postcards all the more authentic.

A common response to the town from viewers is, what's so special about this place that it has enjoyed national attention for so long? The letters often go on to explain that the writer's small town, after all, has exactly the same kind of characters, businesses, and events. So, why don't I come to Fill-In-The-Blank and do a story on its water dowser, or ethnic festival, or problems with natural disasters?

"Why don't you come to Centerville?" they write indignantly. "There's a lot of history in Centerville!"

In a way, letters like that are exactly what I want. They prove my point that every little town is like every other little town and that this wonderful communality is what makes us special. We constitute real, typical America, as opposed to the horrors, ugliness, and villains that bring so many other communities to television news.

"Look around you!" I want to scream. "What is wonderful about my little town is precisely what is wonderful about yours! When I write an essay about the Danish festival in Dannebrog, I am writing about the Greek festival, or Swedish festival, or Latino festival in yours! And what stinks about Dannebrog is probably what stinks about your town! Let's all rise up and throw out the hypocrites, thieves, drug dealers, and religious zealots. Out with them! The

Founding Fathers would have wanted it that way!" The founding fathers of Dannebrog. The founding fathers of Centerville. The founding fathers of America.

Of course Centerville has a lot of history. Dannebrog has a lot of history. Every town and village has a lot of history. In fact, there is no place that doesn't have its full share of history. No person or family that doesn't have history.

Same with our local characters. Of course there's no one like Dan, or Bondo, or Eric, or Dee. At least not in my experience. That's why I'm in Dannebrog, after all. And yet I know that characters of equivalent wit, humor, good spirit, and idiosyncrasy are universal.

I see Don Hochstetler almost every day. He is the mayor of this burg as far as I'm concerned, no matter whom the dopes who vote elect. He is a machinist, hog farmer, well dowser and driller, plumber, and mechanic. I often wonder what will happen to this town if anything happens to Don, because he's the only one who knows where all the water and sewer lines are! When I took up tractor mechanics a few years ago, it was Don I turned to for information, instruction, and rescue, and he has never turned me down. Which isn't to say he doesn't have opinions of his own: as one friend so wonderfully put it, "Don is the kind of guy who'd argue with a compass!"

The Dowser of Dannebrog

I don't know how many Postcards Don showed up in, but the one that focused directly on him dealt with his role as our town's water dowser. It's not at all unusual to see Don somewhere around town or out in the rural countryside, striding with determination, holding in front of him a forked hackberry stick. Someone must be looking for a new well, we know.

When I did the Postcard on Don and his work as a dowser, or water witch, I expected a flood of mail from detractors, and I got it. "Nonsense," they snorted. "Foolishness," "pseudo-science," "claptrap," "superstition." The reason I wasn't surprised, I suppose, is that I had my own doubts, the same doubts. I'm an educated, sophisticated, professorial kind of guy. I know that it's only a matter of common sense that waving a stick four or five feet above the ground has absolutely nothing to do with what sort of water reservoirs lie 100 feet below! You don't need to be a hydrological genius to figure that one out.

But while we were taping our story, I thought that just for fun, while we had Don at work, maybe I'd— well, just . . . uh, give it a try myself. So, Don cut a stick for me and had me stroll across the main street through town a couple times. He knew there was a water main not far below the pavement and so it wouldn't take a particularly sensitive dowser to pick up the vibrations, or emanations, or auras, or whatever the hell it is that's supposed to affect the stick.

I took the stick, held it as Don instructed, and began my walk. Gulp. Despite my best efforts (tight grip, firm step, skeptical mind) the stick twisted and turned downward—right above the water main. I turned and walked back. Down it went again. I walked in another direction. Nothing. Turned 180 degrees and walked back, and aha! The stick dipped just as it had when I crossed the water main. Clearly, the stick dipped at random and . . .

"That's where the line runs into my house," said Eric. Whoops. Guess it wasn't exactly "at random."

At my farm, it was the same thing. The stick clearly dipped at certain places when Don went across them, and then it did again when I walked across. As I have learned since, even though dowsing makes no sense whatsoever, even the most cynical scientists wind up at least wondering what the heck is going on when they give it a try themselves, unless they choose to disregard even the most obvious evidence.

Don't bother to tell me I'm an idiot. I'll just ask you if you've tried it. If you haven't, I won't give you the time of day. If you have, well, you will apologize to me. Take my advice before you snarl: give it a try yourself first.

Unpredictable Performances

The second surprise was that Don, not exactly shy but certainly not a performer, was one of our best on-camera talents in our 10 years of shooting. He seemed perfectly at ease, even when asked to walk through the same steps repeatedly or answer the same question a dozen times. He was a television whiz!

On the other hand, Lyle Fries, our rural mail carrier, was exactly the opposite. Lyle is about the most gregarious, loquacious storyteller around, so we thought we had a natural when we set up an ambush to interview Lyle while doing our story on farm dogs. We set up the camera at my mailbox, out on the highway at the end of our lane. You could almost set your watch by Lyle, so we knew we wouldn't have to wait long. I had my questions well in mind. Lyle came over the hill and around the bend, dropped off mail at the Blakes, our neighbors across the road, and pulled up to our box.

I briefly explained what we were up to and asked, "Lyle, as rural mail carrier, you must know just about every dog in the area . . ."

"Uh, yeah, maybe. No, not really . . ." he said in a voice so quiet we could hardly hear him.

"Well, I'll bet you've had a lot of interesting encounters with dogs when you invade their territory, huh, Lyle?" I tried again.

Long silence . . . "Uh, not really. No. Not really."

By this time sweat was popping out on my brow. "Tell us just one story about an interesting dog you've known during your many years carrying mail on this route, Lyle."

Really long silence . . . "Uh, can't think of any right now . . ."

Jeez, Lyle . . .

Bud edged up behind me and tried to help by whispering a couple more questions in my ear. "Are there times when it's safer to stay in your car when you're delivering mail? Do folks ever bring their dogs along with them when they come out to the road to get their mail? Do you ever have trouble with dogs when you go up to houses with mail?"

I tried those questions. Lyle sweat. Lyle clutched. Lyle had nothing to say. Nothing. Absolutely nothing. Not a sentence. Nothing. The camera might just as well have been a flamethrower aimed at him.

It was at that point that Izzy, Dan, Bud, and I invented a device we would use regularly over the next dozen years: the Friesometer. A Ten on the Friesometer means that our interviewee has matched Lyle's remarkable performance, giving us not a single inch of useable footage. A Zero means that our on-camera friend did a pretty good job, giving us some good lines, useable footage. On rare occasions we have even had some negative readings (which is to say, terrific interviewees) who virtually knock the needle on the Friesometer off the peg! So far, however, no one has outdone Lyle on the positive side with his big ten-out-of-ten.

As it turns out, paralysis is pretty much a standard response to a television camera for most people. It closes them down just as surely as if there were a sign on the front saying "One word and you die!"

Eric is one of my best friends in town, and one of the reasons I have always been attracted to him is his wit, quick humor, perfect timing, marvelous eloquence, great mind for the perfect story. Not on television. Eric has always been grumpily cooperative when we've needed him on camera, or needed to set up some shots in his tavern on Dannebrog's main street, but with Eric it's another case of "Camera on, poise gone!"

Over the years I've tried to include my entire circle of friends in my Postcards from Nebraska, not only to give them a chance to bask in the glories of fame, but because I wanted America to know why I love this place so much. Mel Grim, proprietor of the town's service station, and his successors, Al and LaVon Schmitt, have fallen to the other end of the scale; a little nervous when the tape rolls but pretty darn good on camera—sometimes even terrific.

Dee Steffenhagen always agitated for more camera time, but the fact of the matter is that we always had to sneak up on her when we needed her presence. Given any warning at all, she would show up dressed as if she were going to a formal dinner at the White House— not exactly the sort of thing one expects from a small-town waitress and cook, no matter how good a friend she has been all these years.

We called on good friends Dan and Bondo a dozen times or so, and they were always ready to go. A trifle stiff, perhaps, but not bad for a plumber and an auto body man! Dan showed up in a dozen Postcards, most notably one on fishing over at Lyle Fries's pond and another on the day the birds all leave for the winter. Bondo was a standout in our piece on the baseball strike; our point in that essay being that, well, in a town like Dannebrog, a major league baseball strike is a minor league tempest in a very small teapot. Frankly, no one cares. The media were filled with the disaster of a major league baseball strike. Here, it could have been a shutout of the sushi industry. Who cares?

We finally reached the point where, if we were doing a story on a very local topic but of general interest and needed a good line or two from a local character, we automatically called up Dennis "Bondo" Adams. And he never let us down. He was in fact the star of a Postcard I did on the annual day of the year when the men of this region take over the kitchens to prepare food; not for the table but for the pickup truck, tavern, or hunting trip. Jerky. Venison jerky, goose jerky, elk jerky, maybe even skunk jerky.

At one point in our taping, for example, I asked the assembled jerky makers if they used different recipes. Bondo jarred us all into laughter with his answer: "You bet. Some people prefer less hair in theirs than others." Another good line in that piece came from Marty Hargens. I asked how long jerky will last, and Marty said, "Depends on who knows you have some."

My real regret when I think about the town's characters is that the best ones were gone by the time we started to send the Postcards from Nebraska—most notably, Rod Hat and Bumps Nielsen. Boy, would I have liked to have had them on camera. On second thought, I suppose they would have been another one of those nasty surprises—a big TEN on the Friesometer. Still, I wish you could have met Bumps and Rod. You would have liked them. I did.

Football

I hate collegiate football. Big college football, that is. Big 8, Big 10, Big 12, big baloney, big crapola, big fraud, big stupidity. I think it is an idiotic, brutal game played by small-time criminals and loved by big-time fools. Which opinion makes me a real popular fellow in Nebraska.

Even football enthusiasts are astonished by the virulence of Nebraska football fans; here it is not a game, it is seriously a religion, and a shallow faith it is. Those of us who don't happen to worship the current cast of barn-size felons playing for the University of Nebraska are invited, not in jest, to leave the state. Quickly.

Now there are exceptions. I almost wish there weren't. It would be easier for people like me to despise the whole mess if there weren't good folks tangled up in it. I think of a lineman named Tom Morrow, for example, who was in one of my classes when I was a faculty member at the University. He was doggedly insistent on doing all of his own work in class in explicit defiance of the custom of "tutors" nursing illiterates through a minimal academic program. And he did well. I admired him. Still do. I can't imagine how you can hold down a job as a professional athlete—and that's what the players are—and still excel as a scholar. You've never heard of Tom Morrow, I suspect. His kind are not heroes in Nebraska.

I also resent another former football-player student of mine, Mark Engler. He was a standout football player, and a darned good student. As of this writing, he is also the superintendent of Nebraska's Homestead National Monument, a tribute to the Homestead Act, on the site of the very first homestead in our nation. Mark is bright, interesting, thoroughly decent, articulate . . . all of the things I've learned not to expect from our (hahahahahahaha) player-scholars. So, why does that annoy me? Good guys like Mark spoil my rants, that's why.

My own unpleasant secret, I suppose, is that I'm jealous. I attended the University of Nebraska a long time ago. A couple football players were fraternity brothers and friends of mine. And I envied them. But let's face it: football at the University of Nebraska is for professionals. It is not a student activity. It has nothing to do with students. The players are not students; students don't play football.

And let's face it too—I'm not very coordinated, not all that aggressive, not particularly ambitious, a little lazy even. My legs are short, my pain-level low, my coordination is, uh, modest.

Probably none of that would have made any difference, but my first teaching job was at a little college in Blair, Nebraska: Dana. And yet, as small as it is, Dana was a revelation for me. A few Saturday afternoons each fall we all walked over to the football field. There were no fences, no reserved seats, no skyboxes for high rollers, not even a ticket booth, because there was no admission.

We spectators, students, and faculty sat on a hillside and watched our students (STUDENTS!) play a game (A GAME!) against some other small college, usually losing. There they were, students from my classes-good students. The best poet at our school played center, in fact.

They played, usually losing, and then they laughed, had a party with a keg of beer, and got a good night's sleep so they could study Sunday for their Monday classes. And I realized, damn, I could have played football at Dana! This is the *game* of football. This is the way it should be. Fun, not a business. Students, not semi-professionals. Gentlemen, not brutes. I'd been robbed: I attended the University of Nebraska.

Anyway, I ended up doing three Postcards from Nebraska on football. And they were some of my favorites because I got to get as close to expressing my opinions as I could with the little power I had.

The first piece was in response to the constant barrage of mail, calls, and conversations I got that I should deal with Nebraska football as a Postcard. I knew that wouldn't be easy, because, as you can clearly see, I don't have much good to say about it. But I didn't want to be a complete mud thrower.

So I tried to find a good side, and I think I did—the role that football plays in bringing our state together. In giving people, somehow unable to find anything else productive to do with their energies, something relatively harmless in which they can express their love for Nebraska, their enthusiasm for life, their need for a larger community. Something to be proud of for those whose lives are empty of imagination or sensitivity for things of real value. Okay, that's a sad commentary, but maybe it's a virtue. I'm trying to be a sweetheart here.

So, we followed a Cornhusker football-fan family through its fanatical devotion, the trip to Lincoln, preparations for the game, the pre-game lunch, the trip to the stadium, their enthusiasm for the game. It wasn't enough for the few fans who also watch "Sunday Morning," but it was about the best face I could put on what I consider a sad situation.

Six-Man Football

I had my chance to express a more positive vision of the game (but not the Cornhuskers) in two other Postcards, both some of my favorites from the list appended to the end of this book. One story was from my own new life on the rural Plains, six-man football.

Elba is a little town just north of Dannebrog. It is not a consolidated school, so it doesn't have enough students for a full football team of 11 players with backup players, special squads, specialists and all that, so it belongs to a conference where abbreviated teams play.

Yes, every moment I was thinking, just as you suspect, "Damn, I wish I could have gone to a high school like Elba's and played football myself."

The third football story was Bud Lamoreaux's. Lou Sabin, former coach of Army and Northwestern, the Patriots, the Broncos, and the Buffalo Bills, had wound up coaching at a tiny state school in Peru, Nebraska, and was on the brink of winning a championship. When Bud first brought it up and sent me some newspaper clippings, I was not at all enthusiastic. Bud covers a lot of the sports pieces for "Sunday Morning," and frankly, this looked like just another one of those to me. I told him I just couldn't see that this was a story for me. Well, by now you know how I feel about college football! Bud doesn't know Nebraska, doesn't understand me, and well . . .

But it's hard to find stories from way down in the most remote southeast corner of the state, and it is a beautiful landscape; rugged, hilly, wooded, all of which was certain to be even more dramatic when draped in autumn foliage, so, we did it.

And the scenery was spectacular. And the football team won its game (not a big issue, but nice, since we were there on their home field). But the main thing was that Lou Sabin was wonderful. Here was a man of national stature, stuck in a tiny apartment in an obscure Nebraska river town, coaching at an insignificant college, in a minor league. Lou was past his prime, way past his prime, and I dreaded the thought that we might be doing a story on a burnt out Old Fart, thrown away, a shell of his former self, a has-been.

Lou Rules

Far from it. Lou Sabin was vibrant. He was treated like a hero by the folks in the local coffee shop. People waved and yelled encouragement to him from their pickup trucks as he walked the streets of Peru. Wherever he went, he was still the center of attention, and it was clear to all of us that he loved every moment of it.

His team loved him too—worshiped him. As they said themselves, this was their chance, even at tiny Peru State College, to play for a great coach: *Lou Sabin!* And he worked. And he worked them. It wasn't as if he'd mellowed or softened in his dotage. If anything, he was even tougher than he'd been in the NFL. He screamed at them, he cursed, he pushed them (literally and metaphorically). It wasn't even as if Lou was just grateful to be working in football somewhere in Nebraska. No, here was a man who clearly worked just as hard here as he did when he was in the big stadiums of America.

It was a real revelation for me. Lou Sabin was not in football for money or power or all the other slimy things I believe now dominate even the collegiate game. He was in this game for the game. He loved football and football players; it made no difference whatsoever to him that these were not major leaguers, and never would be major leaguers in all but one or two exceptional cases every other decade or so. It simply didn't matter to Lou Sabin. It was still football, and he was still Lou Sabin, and that's absolutely all that mattered.

It was the kind of story I love, one where I learn something new to me. My mind wasn't changed about collegiate football; in fact, I resent the current distortion of it even more now that I've seen through Lou Sabin what it could be. But my mind sure was changed about Lou. What a guy. A real man. God, what would happen if Lou Sabin could save collegiate football from the zealots?! We'll never know.

And maybe that's what defines my own obverse relationship with football. Everyone in Nebraska—every average person—mindlessly embraces it, no matter how pernicious, ugly, and deceitful it is. So I make a point and show of disdaining it. Any average person in Lou Sabin's position, at his age, would have, should have been just as done with football, as it seemed to be with him. But he wouldn't follow those rules: instead, he let his enthusiasm burn even brighter than ever. My kind of guy.

God bless you, Lou Sabin. I wish I could play football under your leadership. In a perfect world, I would.

Birds

At this very moment, I am sitting in my cluttered office, looking out winter-stained windows, across trees shattered and tattered by another hard winter. But it's okay—the sky is filled with birds, so spring can't be far away. Here in central Nebraska, March is a busy time of year for the birds. The ponds and river bottoms are filled with snow and Canada geese and sandhill cranes; flocks of robins and mourning doves are passing through, stopping on their way along our river.

I love watching the birds, I love the sounds, I love the season, but most of all, I love the fact that the birds really don't give a damn about us ground-bound folks. We are of no consequence in this truly grand scheme, and I wish this were the case more often with the trivialities of mankind. The birds have cosmic matters to attend to these days, and can't therefore even spare the time and energy it would take to look down on us.

Over the years we sent three Postcards from Nebraska dealing with birds—well, more than that if you count our own ducks and chickens, the ostrich farmers, that kind of thing, but three that dealt with wild birds. Perhaps the most predictable were those about the cranes and their annual migration through Nebraska's Platte valley and the bald eagles' annual stopover.

I grew up in Nebraska and traveled the roads of the state with unusual frequency, I think. But somehow I missed the sandhill cranes until 20 years ago when I bought my land along the Middle Loup River. I was a grown man when I mentioned to someone in the parking lot of the Cozad public schools that I had never seen the cranes and wouldn't know what I was looking at if I ever saw one. Or heard one.

"Oh, you'll know when you hear them—and there's never just one," my friend laughed, so I started listening. I heard and saw them, and I knew what I was hearing and seeing. The peculiar b-r-r-r-r-r and great wheeling mass is indeed unmistakable. And once I saw them, my eyes and ears found them everywhere. Fields I had driven by a thousand times without glancing at sideways were suddenly filled with the four- and five-foot-tall, regal creatures. Great flocks whirled on either side of the high-ways and over our farm. Lines and vees thousands of feet long spun northward, or southward, depending on the season. The air was filled night and day with the whirring and buzzing. How could they possi-bly have always been here and I had missed them? It simply didn't seem reasonable, made no sense. But there they were, right where I used to look and see nothing.

Good thing. Now, as competing interests struggle for the water and land the cranes have enjoyed for all time, to grow yet one more bushel of corn we don't need or for water to wash another automo-bile we could do without, it is possible that I came to see the mag-nificence of the great avian migrations just about the time they are to be wiped out for all time.

God, I hope not. Frankly, I would rather see beer production stopped for a month and all interstate highways closed than to know my grandchildren might not see the wonder of another primeval migration of the cranes and geese.

If there were ever a time for ecoterrorists, this might be it. I have always thought that if I found out I had a terminal disease but had a month more to live, I would love to die at the helm of a fast boat loaded with explosives, slamming into the front loading slide of a whaling ship. I would go to my death gladly knowing I had sunk one of those blasphemies.

Maybe I should save my fury for dropping an overpass on Nebraska's I-80 during crane migration. One explosives-loaded car could divert a week's worth of drivers who would then have to drive through crane country and actually see what life is about.

I think about it.

Bald Eagles

Then I calm down and soothe my passions with the idea that there may be hope even without drastic action. After all, there was a time not all that long ago when we wondered if we would ever again see bald eagles, our national bird.

I once climbed Courthouse Rock out in Nebraska's panhandle to try to understand an old Indian legend about the site. It's not really much of a climb—Nebraska doesn't have a lot of alpine terrain, after all! The story was that a group of one tribe (Pawnee, the legend often goes) were cornered atop the wedge-shaped slab, and another tribal party (Lakota, perhaps, or Cheyenne) simply settled in at the base of the wedge to starve out their prey. The Pawnee, however, cut their leggings and other clothing into strips and wove a rope, which they then used to drop down the steep, backside of the promontory. I thought I'd like to climb the rock and see how likely the legend was.

I camped overnight at the Bridgeport, Nebraska, campground (and was, by the way, kept awake most of the night by a rowdy, loud party of Canada geese that were also camped there for the night). So I was on the rock before dawn, clambering up the sloped side. It was easy enough a climb and when I reached the summit, I eased over the south edge to appraise the drop and assess the feasibility of rappelling down on a rope of minced leather clothing. It is a substantial drop, and very sheer, but the legend could conceivably have a historical foundation, I eventually concluded, but not right away.

I didn't have time to do a lot of thinking, as it turned out, because as I eased my head over the cliff's brink, there, immediately below me, perhaps 10 yards away, was a beautiful golden eagle, the first eagle I had ever seen outside a zoo. He whipped around, piercing me with his eyes, and dropped off his perch to strafe the valley below us, screaming . . . in surprise? I don't know what kind of sound I made, but my astonishment left me shaking. I lay there on the warm rock, disoriented by the eagle's accusation. The laser-sharpness of his eyes has never left me since.

Perhaps I should note that I was so exhilarated by the eagle, I decided I would also climb Jail Rock, a few hundred yards away from Courthouse Rock, but considerably steeper, with no easy slope up any side. I made the climb and stood atop the prominence, looking for the eagle again, when I noticed a thunderstorm approaching rapidly from the south. And here I was, the highest thing in any direction for maybe 20 miles! My father was struck by lightning when he was a lad, so it's a part of family history.

Then I couldn't figure out how to get down. It's one thing after all to climb a cliff when the handholds are right there in front of your eyes, but quite another to descend, trying to locate footholds with the eyes in your toes. Then it started to rain and lightning, making the descent all the more urgent, all the more uncertain. It was a long day. It's as frightened as I have ever been. At the end of it I was totally exhausted, thoroughly drained emotionally from fear, awe, relief, and suspicions of my own stupidity. And the magnificence of nature. Days like that are important.

But I had seen my eagle. And for many years, that was the sum total of my eagle experiences. The next occasion was just as surprising, just as unlikely. I was sitting at a table in my old log cabin down by the Loup River bottoms grading semester mid-term exams. My children Joyce, Jenny, and Chris were with me. I don't recall what they were doing but they were near the house, or perhaps in the house, with me. It was mid-winter, probably December, the end of the first university semester.

I happened to glance up from a paper I was looking at and as if in slow motion, an enormous bird flew slowly down the slough directly in front of the window. It was slow enough that there was no mistake—it was a bald eagle, 20 feet above the ground, 40 feet from our house. And yet it was utterly so impossible a sight that my eyes refused to accept it, and it was too fast to let me verify if this was reality or some sort of hallucination (to which I am not given, by the way).

I leaped from my chair, sending it crashing across the floor and tore out the front door running as fast as my fat, short legs would carry me in the direction the bird—or B-1 bomber, perhaps—had flown. I was screaming to my children, "Come onChrisJenJoyce, comeoncomeoncomeon . . . eagleeagleeagle . . . runrunrun!!" I could hear them behind me, running, probably terrified about what the hell this new paternal crisis was about.

We ran west along the trees lining the slough and then down through a dry crossing and out onto a clearing we've always called Goat Island. There, high on a huge old cottonwood leaning out over the river, was an unidentifiable figure. An apparition. We stopped and stared. The Thing was enormous, too big to be in a tree. Our eyes, having never seen anything like this in a tree anywhere let alone here on our own farm, rejected the image. We looked again. We gasped our speculation.

"It's a bald eagle . . ."

"Can't be . . ."

"But it is a bald eagle . . ."

It was only 30 or 40 yards away, clearly visible, unobstructed, but our eyes and our minds had trouble processing the wonder of it.

Then it spread its great wings and flew low over the river toward the west, and the four of us stood there utterly speechless from the magnificence of the gift we had just been given. We had seen an eagle. A bald eagle. On our own land, at our own river, in our tree.

The rest of our day was given over to describing over and over, again and again, what we had seen. We wanted to know every detail each of the others had locked in their minds. We wanted to etch permanently in our own minds what we had seen.

After all, we might never, any of us, see that sight again.

Thanks to all The Powers that control such things. We have seen it again, many times. As many as nine eagles whirling over our home at the same time, two at a time fighting over a fish high above us, pairs, singles, young and mature. We were moving an old house onto our farm once for my artist-wife Linda to use as a studio. We looked up, and there was a bald eagle circling overhead. A sign? Well . . .

Now there are even eagles nesting, laying, and fledging young within miles of our home. In fact, it is the unusual winter month that we don't enjoy an eagle-sighting.

For my eagle Postcard, Bud, Dan, Izzy, and I traveled an hour away from my farm to a dam site near Lexington, Nebraska, where openings in the ice and a constant supply of fish now draw dozens, even hundreds of eagles each winter. We got our shots of eagles diving, soaring, bending trees with their weight, and I like to think it was one of the prettiest picture postcards we sent in our 10 years.

Marking the Migrations

My favorite essay about birds however, was much simpler, much more humble. Actually, it was not so much about birds as about my plumber buddy Dan Selden, a man of modest education who, nonetheless, has taught this old professor a lot over the years.

Our story centered on an actual event, a day that Dan came by our house and stood there smiling a goofy smile when I opened the door, asking, "Well, did you notice?"

"Did I notice what?"

"What do you hear?"

I listened. I strained. I heard nothing.

"I don't hear anything," I said.

"Exactly," Dan said. "The birds are gone."

He went on to explain to this very skeptical audience that there is one day when all the birds leave in the fall and another when they all come back in the spring. I know that Dan knows a lot about nature, having grown up on the farm and out here in the country, and I am a city boy and don't know a lot, but come on! "No, it's true," he insisted. "I woke up this morning and the birds were gone. They left early this morning."

"So, what do they do? Have a little conference? Arrive at a consensus? Buy their tickets together? Check their calendars? Set their alarms?"

"I don't know, Mr. Smart-Ass Professor, but you'll have to admit, the birds are all gone."

And they were. And the next spring Dan showed up one morning shortly after sunrise, a grin of triumph on his face, and announced, "What do you hear?"

Our farm, silent the day before, was now a cacophony. The birds were back. I had to admit that, well, he just might be right, but . . . I don't know. Of course, since that time, Dan may or may not show up here at our place (he tries to come by every Sunday for coffee and "Sunday Morning"). But I do know he'll be here at least twice, Sunday or not, standing at the door or gate, ear tipped to the bottomlands or sky, eyebrow raised, saying, "Hear anything?" And either we do or we don't. The birds are gone, or the birds are back.

The lesson for me, and for Postcard viewers, was not about birds. It was about the rural wisdom of people like Dan who listen and watch and learn things the rest of us in the cities and universities miss all too often. I'm glad I have Dan to remind me of that, at least twice a year.

Between Birds and Sky
and Passage . . .

I'm not sure whether my favorite Postcard from Nebraska was the one with Union Pacific steam engine #3985 or the one with Tom and Gloria Kammerer of Leshara, Nebraska. It was one of the few where I actually came close to being able to tell the story my way without the producers' utterly idiotic notion that every story must start with the punchline, which is actually a tired requirement of print journalism from a half century ago.

So, this Postcard began with a picture of Tom on his tractor, doing some minor fieldwork, shredding weeds alongside a cornfield, as I recall. Then we sat at Tom and Gloria's kitchen table, sipping lemonade and talking about farming; yields, market prices, fertilizer types and applications. The conversation was edited just right, so things approached the ragged edge of boring before I said something like, "But sometimes Tom puts aside his farm cap [image of seed cap being put onto a mud porch clothes peg] and puts on . . . his helmet." [Image of Tom sliding on his Darth Vader helmet as he crawls into the cockpit of his F-16 Fighting Falcon].

Tom Kammerer, like so many other farmers I know, is not a backwoods clodhopper. Farming is high-tech these days, and so people like Tom and Gloria are not only extraordinarily skilled in agricultural technology, they are quite at home in other areas of the high-tech world too. And so, on weekends Tom is a pilot with the Iowa Air National Guard, stationed at Sioux City, Iowa.

That was our story, and it was a good one. But it was not, in all honesty, the bottom line for me. Much as was the case with Union Pacific #3985, the hidden agenda was that this was another chance to violate Charles Kuralt's dictum against "riding the tricycle."

The offense was so blatant in this case, in fact, I called Charles and told him what I was up to: "Charles, I am going to do a story in which I am going to ride the tricycle," I told him.

"I'm doing a story on a guy who flies, but I'm going to finagle a way to fly with him." There was a long pause on the phone. "Charles," I said, trying to sound pitiful, "It's an F-16 fighter plane, and no matter what you say, I'm going to do this story because I want to ride that plane so bad, I don't care if it kills me."

(There are in fact some details of this particular part of the story that I cannot to this day report fully because some good, kind people went out on a limb for me, taking a real risk in putting an old fat guy into the cockpit of that ferocious beast of an airplane. But as I told Kuralt, and told them, if I were to die in that plane, I would die a very happy man, while if I were not to get to fly in it, I would probably die even sooner, full of regrets and resentments. To a soul they did what it took to get me into the plane!)

Again there was a pause from Kuralt's end of the phone;

I said nothing. Finally Charles sighed a great sigh and said, "F-16, huh? Rog . . . ride that tricycle." It turned out to be one of the greatest days of my life (with the single possible exception, I note when in Linda's company, of our wedding day).

Fixin' to Ride

We arrived in Sioux City early in the day. I had been warned that there would be a morning of orientation before I could fly. It wasn't easy. To begin with, fighter pilots are young, lean, hard athletes. And I, uh, am not. They got the largest flying suit and G-suit (a very tight-fitting suit made to counter the debilitating effects of extreme gravity during hard maneuvers) they could find, and while I did squeeze into the flight suit, there was no way I was going to get the G-suit over this torso.

I once trained to drive formula cars at the Bondurant School of High Performance Driving, then at Sears Point, California; they not only couldn't find a driving suit to fit me, they had to take the sheet metal off a car and get a larger racing body to fit the non-racing body God gave me!

Red-faced (both from embarrassment and the painfully tight flight suit), I spent the morning hanging from parachute straps, squeezing into a flight simulator, and being lectured to, hard, about what I was to do in the event of a mishap. Gulp. There was talk of near-sonic ejections; loosen that strap, drop this one, pull the yellow handle between your legs. Don't ever touch that button, be prepared for this, you may experience that . . .

And oh by the way, here is a large plastic bag you should keep in a shoulder pocket in case you find yourself needing to, well, you'll know.

I finally reached and expressed the same conclusion I had arrived at for any medical problems: "I'm not going to learn all this. I can't remember a single thing you've told me except for pulling the yellow handle. Frankly, I don't care. I just want to fly. If I die, I die happy. I'll sign anything to excuse you from any liability. So, let's cut the crap and crawl into that magic dragon sitting out there on the tarmac!"

The pilot who took me under his wing was Colonel Denny Swanstrom, a wonderful, mellow guy who has become a friend of mine, I am proud to say. (I kid him to this day about being my co-pilot and how our flight was what made him decide to retire just a couple years later.) We were in a two-seater F-16, a relatively rare training version of the F-16. Tom Kammerer was in another, and two other pilots and planes filled out our quarter.

So how do we tape in planes where there is barely room for the pilot (and in the case of Denny Swanstrom, his passenger) not to mention a cameraman, soundman, and producer? Well, there are two ways to do that. Izzy taped a "lipstick" camera to the control panel of Tom's plane, so we had a head-on image of him. And Iz, Dan, and Bud shot with their cameras from the platform of a refueling tanker.

The KC-135 refueling tanker was from the Nebraska Air National Guard unit in Lincoln, of which I was once a member, so it was a matter of dealing with old comrades in arms, almost. The way these things work is that the enormous refueler is jammed full of tons of jet fuel. The F-16 tucks up under the belly of the refueler, within feet of it, at nearly supersonic speeds. A long tube extends from the tail of the refueler, literally flown into position by a crewman lying on his belly in the very tail end of the plane, maneuvering the nozzle to a port on the top of the F-16, immediately behind the huge plastic bubble of a cockpit cover.

That's where I was sitting. That means here we were, flying at incredible speeds, jammed into the cockpit, tucked within feet of a plane the size of a freight train, high above the Nebraska landscape. There was a long tube within arm's length over my head, full of highly flammable fuel, tucking into a socket, right behind my head!

But this is how we did it: Izzy, Bud, and Dan were in the tail end of the plane with the man handling the refueling nozzle and shooting footage of me, just feet away, in the F-16. How close were we? At one point, Iz motioned to me to hold my thumb up in a gesture of approval. I could not only see his signal, I could see his lips saying, "Thumbs up!" That's how close we were.

A thrill? That's what the whole flight was like, three or four hours of unimaginable wonderment. I should have known how it would be from the moment our wheels left Mother Earth. As we sat on the runway waiting for clearance, calibrating instruments, checking all the plane's vitals, Denny asked me over our inter-plane communications system, "Is there anything you want to do while we have this bird in the air?"

"Uh, yeah," I said tentatively, although I'd certainly considered the issue in planning this story. "Er, I've heard these things will go straight up."

"Oh, yeah," Denny said with a laugh in his voice. "She'll go straight up!"

Into the Wild Blue Yonder

When everything was ready for our takeoff, the engine roared and I was crushed back into the seat by incredible power. We were, after all, two very small human beings sitting astride a gigantic engine, as large a dragster as you can imagine, with 25,000 pounds of thrust under the hood.

We had just cleared the runway and pulled up our landing gear when I noticed Denny quickly glance to the sky above him. Uh-oh. And then . . . wham! He pointed her nose straight up and we were heaven-bound on the front end of a Roman candle. I don't know how long we lay there, pointing straight up, but about the time I had had enough, Denny leveled off.

Upside down. UPSIDE DOWN!!! (Later, after landing, as I was crawling on my hands and knees from the plane, I overheard Colonel Swanstrom's crew chief say to him, "Nice takeoff, Colonel." I had to settle for the praise of everyone at the base as they wondered at my empty plastic bag. I came close, but I came down unregurgitated.)

Immediately I sputtered into the microphone that Denny should tell Tom to make the same kind of takeoff, thinking the footage from his lipstick camera would be a real keeper. It was in fact so dramatic, we sat in a motel room later that night literally screaming at the monitor screen. We saw Tom's helmet, like a giant insect face. We saw him working controls. Then suddenly we could see the ground streaming faster and faster alongside him. Then just off the runway, he made that little glance upwards, and then zoooooom! Straight up!

Behind—or, below him, we saw the runway, then the airport, then Nebraska, then the world . . . okay, I exaggerate a little, but not much. The footage was incredible, and virtually made the Postcard.

Once in the air we joined the refueler, perhaps a mile or so to its rear. I wondered aloud into my oxygen mask/microphone, "We're getting pretty close to the refueler, aren't we, Denny?" (I had no idea at this point that we would be hooked to that monster before long, flying in its very shadow!)

"Well, Rog, take a look to your right," Swanstrom said. I did. And again my heart flew into my throat. There, not 10 feet off the end of our wing tips was another F-16. (During the flight I learned that flying in such close formation, pilots do not look ahead. They look at each other. If the lead plane goes into the ground, they all go into the ground. Thing is, the only thing they have to worry about up there is bumping each other. They can't even *see* things they might hit up ahead of them! Most of the time, rather than use their radios, they simply signal back and forth with their hands. They fly so close, they can see each others' fingers!)

We organized our flight, four F-16s and our mother ship, and flew over Tom and Gloria's farm at Leshara, then to Lincoln, where we circled the town I was born in. I directed our formation to my parents' neighborhood; it was my mother's birthday. Later she told me that when we flew our salute over their house, she cried tears of joy. But nothing like the joy I was feeling.

Next we headed west to Grand Island and my current home, doing refueling exercises along the way, giving Izzy plenty of time to get incredible footage of not only the subject of our story, Tom Kammerer, but also of ol' Rog, grinning so wide his teeth and lips extended well behind either side of his head.

At Grand Island we turned northwest, toward Dannebrog. Linda later told me that about this time she was in our backyard. I had warned her that we would be coming over Dannebrog, almost certainly. She said she suddenly noticed the dogs acting very uneasy and heading for their back porch. Then she said the ground began to shake in a peculiar way. Then she said we exploded over the trees at the river, literally at treetop height; that monstrous mother ship with four Star-Wars fighters in tow. She told me that she involuntarily dropped to her knees in astonishment.

Once we had passed over my town, Denny sent the refueler on three other fighters on their way to the west while we circled town again. He put the plane into a very tight circle (it's a small town!) and when we'd completed the 360 degrees asked, "Did you get a good view of the place?"

"Well, uh, no," I admitted. "Somewhere along the way I lost everything."

"Whoops," Denny laughed. "I forgot . . . we couldn't get you into a G-suit." Pressed down into the seat, I had felt my face sag and suddenly it was seconds later and we had circled the town without me along. "I'll take her around again a little looser," he said.

After we had toured the town thoroughly, we gained some altitude. "Can you see the rest of the boys up ahead?" he asked.

"Yeah, I can just make them out," I answered.

"Okay, put your hand on the stick. Feel this?" He moved the stick from side to side, up and down, slowly, easily. The plane responded smoothly. "Got the feel?" He did the maneuvers again. "Okay, hang onto the stick," he instructed. And then, after a pause, "She's yours."

God, it gives me goose pimples just to write it! I was flying that marvelous creature. She was in my hands. I did nothing fancy, I can tell you for a fact, but I can say with all honesty that I had the controls of an F-16.

When we rejoined our comrades and Denny took the controls, we did some other maneuvers (as I recall, I wasn't courageous enough to repeat many of them twice) out over Nebraska's desolate Sandhills landscape, where an accident was unlikely to take innocent victims, and where our noise was not likely to offend a soul.

The Need for Speed

We came alongside the refueler and Denny said that we were going to return to Sioux City so we could watch them land. On one hand, I didn't want this flight ever to end, on the other I wasn't sure at this point how much more my stomach could take. The others signaled farewell to us, we waved, and then there was another surprise in store for ol' Rog: Denny Swanstrom hit the afterburner and suddenly I was out of commission again. We may have gone straight up again while I was unconscious, I can't be sure.

The footage that Izzy shot from the tanker shows us there one second, and flashing out of sight like a bullet in the next. (Although I should note that the F-16 does not flash like a bullet. It is faster than a bullet!)

As we zipped back to home base, Denny said something that put it all in perspective. He said that he likes to fly over farm landscape because then he can see the mile roads passing beneath him, one every six seconds—at cruising speed, twice that when in a hurry. On the Oregon Trail, wagon trains covered six or seven miles a day. On the interstate, I drive six or seven miles in five or six minutes. With Denny Swanstrom I was covering five or six miles per minute. Following the same path as the pioneers, but making in moments what they traveled in weeks, in hours what they made in months.

The flight was a remarkable day in my long life. But it was everyday for Denny and the others in our flight. In fact, once the CBS boys and I left them, they took off again to make training runs over Wisconsin landscape, pretty much what they would encounter should they wind up over Bosnia.

There is a curious after-note to this story. It is one of the few we ever managed to do a follow-up story on. A couple years after our flight I ran into Denny Swanstrom again, in the unlikely context of the wonderful Cabela's sporting goods store in Kearney, Nebraska. He was there, shopping with a family member, but he told me he had retired from the cockpit and was now pursuing another activity in his life: walking. He had taken up hiking various trails around America, a remarkable transformation from 1000 miles an hour to two or three miles an hour; not at 30,000 feet but at ground level. Not with 25,000 pounds of thrust at the seat of his pants but by the power of his own two feet.

Little wonder I chose to talk with Denny on camera at the very end of my national television career and to do one more Postcard from Nebraska with him. This time in the calm and quiet of a late fall hike.

Sky and Passage

I think it must be a product of my environment (or maybe that I'm a product of my environment) that I am so preoccupied by the sky and its movements. Just last night, as I write this, I dragged my family out to the open pasture land northwest of our house to wonder at the Hale-Bopp comet gleaming above the horizon. Maybe it's because of something I've already shared with you: that I love the idea of cosmic, inexorable workings because it reminds man (at least this man) of where exactly we belong in the scheme of things—not much of anywhere.

My dream, after all, is that of Loren Eiseley's in his wonderful poem, "Watch the Uneasy Landlords." One day the glaciers far to the arctic north will begin adding inches of new ice a year, eventually leading yet once again to great sheets of ice working their way down to the Plains, where they'll scrape off all the trivial garbage of man and recreate the flatlands chronic to this continental interior:

> *Sometimes on winter nights before my window*
> *I lift a hand against the draft and judge if anywhere*
> *far off, far off in cold Sierras of my mind,*
> *in latitudes that lie somewhere above the circle of the pole,*
> *pack ice has swollen, bergs increased,*
> *a wind grown colder, a blue shadow deepened.*
> *The Fifth Ice would be cleansing if it moved,*
> *but will it move in time?*

My favorite movie, by the way, is a Paul Newman film not a single other person alive has ever seen, as far as I can tell, *Quintet*, which tells almost exactly this same story. It would seem that Eiseley and I are not alone in our fantasies!

Part of that great cosmic grinding, of course, is time. I suppose that's ultimately what the glaciers and birds and man and the Plains are all about—time. I take my religion very strongly (and very personally, I might add, so I don't share much of it with others) and time is a good part of the mysteries that move my soul. But my fascination is not just with the enormous and grand sweeps of nature and time; I am dazzled looking at things as modest as a grain of sand or moment of time.

Yes, eons, millennia, even centuries can be astonishing in their scope, in how much they can contain by way of human and historic events. But to me, even a year is a remarkable thing. I am amazed at how much happens in nature in a year, and how much happens in a life in a year. In fact, I think a year is a rather remarkable unit.

I don't believe that a year is noteworthy because it somehow speaks to man, but because man somehow speaks to a year. That is, our life rhythms are, understandably, set to the passage of 365 sunrises and sunsets. After all, every human being for all time has had to live with this system, so it only stands to reason that it might have made some dent on our psyches, rather than, as arrogant religionists would have it, that we've had an impact on it.

So, I make a point of paying some attention to the years as they move along. I try to follow my Omaha brother's admonition to live each moment of every day as if it were a prayer of gratitude, but I make a special point of remembering the larger things, specifically, on equinoxes and solstices. (Before you get excited, I don't worship the sun; I use it as a reminder of all the grand movements around me, and my—well, all of our—insignificance in that movement.)

So, the morning of every solstice and equinox I get up before dawn and walk up behind our house to the top of the highest hill. There I look out over the river and valley, our home, my family, my state and the Plains, and I make a special note of my gratitude to all those things that have so graced my life. My prayer then, as always, is "By what grace am I here?" And then, because Linda is so enormous a part of my gratitude, "By what grace is she mine?" And then my children . . . Chris, Joyce, Jenny, Antonia. And then my German family and my Omaha family. And my friends. And my life and all the good fortune I've had in it . . .

That's it. Not much of a prayer, I know, but there it is, and it seems to be enough.

And I go on New Year's Eve too. I don't know why. You would think that the solstices and equinoxes would be enough, but I feel the need to go up my hill on New Year's Eve, my one nighttime foray, to give thanks then. And to think about what has transpired the past year and to anticipate what will happen the next. Not to guess, because I have found that reality is far too preposterous to anticipate, but to think.

It's then that I mull over what a remarkable period a year is. It is enormously long, long enough to be a strain on the memory. What happened a year ago seems a long time ago—the pain and joy almost gone. And yet it is no time at all. A year ago is almost like yesterday. New Year's Eve, therefore, is like a fulcrum in time, a point on which the beam of time balances.

And I love that. Sure, it's just another night. Yeah, a day or two this way or that, or a week, wouldn't really make much of a difference. New Year's Eve is just another night that has been arbitrarily designated as special, probably by mistake of calendar and faith. But it is a convenient night for me to remember, and I do.

One For the Ages

I was surprised when Bud went along with my request to do a story about my New Year's Eve feelings and rituals. It is very personal, very esoteric, very . . . well, very romantic. But we did the story. We had our share of problems shooting it. We put Iz Bleckman in my tractor bucket to get a high-angle shot, but the bucket kept creeping (and creaking) down. And we all got cactus spines in our shoes. It was cold and it was miserable.

But there was a surprise: a sunset so stunningly glorious that when we reviewed our film, it looked like a camera trick, some sort of special effects or computer-generated trickery. The clouds, sun, sky, and earth combined to make an image that looked like something from an alien world in a sci-fi movie.

A lot of viewers saw it and were amazed, or dubious. They thought it was a video stunt, or perhaps a cinematographical accident perhaps. I looked at the images we had captured on tape and was amazed too; but not dubious. I knew it was a stunt—a cosmic stunt—and I knew it wasn't an accident. That was as close as I have come to discussing my religion in my "Sunday Morning" Postcards from Nebraska.

Another "time" piece that probably no one but me thinks of as a "time" piece was the story about prehistoric animal tracks frozen in rock in Toadstool Park in northwestern Nebraska. David Nixon, an old friend of mine, was curator at the Trailside Museum in Chadron, Nebraska, and was our guide on that ferociously hot July day. But it wasn't the heat that made my head spin; it was the remarkable elasticity of time that sent me reeling.

Millions of years ago some animals, many of which have been extinct for intervening millions of years, walked down a river bed, perhaps in a migration. They left their tracks, which were then petrified, turned to stone, covered, buried, pitched about in eons-long geological crunches, then raised and exposed once again to the light of day. David showed us the tracks and identified the animals. Perhaps the most moving to me were the tracks of one rhino that had a bad right back leg. He was dragging his toes just a bit.

To me this made that set of tracks individual. One animal, millions of years ago. One set of footprints. One moment in time, frozen for millions of years, visited by us, frozen on tape again. Wow. What does that say about time, mortality, and immortality? It says too much for me to understand.

Soup Contest

I guess you've noticed that I like to eat. Heaven knows, plenty of you have written over the years commenting on my girth (and eventual diminution of it). Well, yes, I do enjoy eating, and so it's not surprising that Postcards from Nebraska have shown me eating Mexican, Greek, and Indian food, steak and potatoes, breakfast, lunch, and supper, either off of pickup truck hoods or in fancy dining cars rolling along railroad right of ways. Food is not only a source of comfort, pleasure, and nutrition to me, it has also been a focus of my academic attention over the years, because I've worked with anthropological aspects of what we eat.

Ultimately, I suppose that's why I so thoroughly enjoyed the Postcard from Nebraska we did about a humble soup contest at Eric's Tavern in Dannebrog. All those things I love about food were rolled into this one simple idea that seemed to be little more than a small-town way for people to show off their culinary skills.

Actually, the piece was almost archeological. There was a time when, about once a month, folks in town got together and brought dishes to Eric's for a potluck dinner. It was good food and good company and was a very popular occasion for all of us. But a lot of things happened over the years to diminish the luster of the family gathering.

Eric grew less and less charmed with the business, and therefore less and less charming; a lot of the genuine characters of the town left, or died, or fell out of favor. I suppose I hoped somewhere deep in my heart that perhaps if we revived the old monthly gatherings on this one occasion for television, the old custom might reestablish roots and flourish again.

Didn't happen. But the gathering was fun, and what's more important—a lot more important—we wound up with seven huge pots of potato soup (my favorite!) sitting on the bar, steaming, inviting, ladles at the ready for sampling.

The evening turned out to be a remarkable culinary event:

it was not as if there were good soup and bad soup, or even fair soup and not-so-fair soup. There was nothing but totally superb soup—gallons of it, all different, all potato. I was in heaven; as they say around here, like a hog at a self-feeder.

A Delicious Dilemma

A problem I had not anticipated arose as the evening drew toward a close. I sensed that the cooks were accepting this event as a real contest, and that they expected an announcement of some sort of results. And they expected it to come from me, the putative judge. Well, these cooks are all friends of mine, and one is my own wife. I began to understand the sort of jeopardy in which I had placed myself. If I awarded first prize to my wife, everyone else would see this as a clear case of family loyalty; if I didn't, I would sleep alone for weeks, if not months. If not forever.

I thought about an announcement of an across-the-board tie. Producer Bud said no. I thought about using the Lincolnesque locution that the soups were all so good, that "each is better than the rest." Bud wouldn't hear of that either. I weighed my potential for survival if I simply made a break for the door!

Bud and the others finally made it clear that I would have to announce a winner. And so I did. And I made the mistake of awarding the Dannebrog Potato Soup Championship to Lowell Lane. Not only a male, but curator of our village dump. Well, his was the best soup of the lot. That's why I awarded him first prize. I wanted to avoid any hint of favoritism, nepotism, or politics. And Lowell's soup was clearly the best.

I'm still hearing about my choice. And now I know—I should have gone ahead and indulged in favoritism, nepotism, and politics and given the purple ribbon to Linda. Everyone would have understood. But I certainly shouldn't have given the award to the cook with the best soup.

When in doubt, survive.

Long Ago . . .
Very Long Ago!

A continual question, not only from viewers but also from friends and neighbors, has been, "Do you ever run out of ideas?" And my persistent answer has been, "No."

I have always been a curious person. Professionally I have been a folklorist and anthropologist, a linguist and researcher. So, all my life I've been preparing for the finding and investigation of precisely the kind of things I've dealt with in Postcards from Nebraska. In fact, only rarely have I had to come up with something entirely new; most of the time my Postcards from Nebraska covered issues I've dealt with before in my life. Sometimes a long time before.

My two essays about paleontology (old bones) were straight out of my childhood wonder. In a piece about the gravel pits that pock Nebraska, once the home of the world's largest "silica mine," or sand pit, I related the story about the time I was fishing—or rather, supposed to be fishing—with my Dad and my uncles Al and Elzie. I suppose I was eight or nine years old and, like most kids that age, I soon grew tired of being quiet and watching bobbers, so I drifted off to an abandoned sandpit not far from the little creek where we were, uh, fishing.

In a pile of pit refuse (rocks too large or jagged to be used on roads or in construction), I found a bone. It appeared to be old and, like kids then and now, I had visions of dinosaurs. So I took it home and on one of my next trips to the State Museum on the University of Nebraska campus, a place I spent many, many Saturdays of my youth, I knocked at the door of one of the staff. I think it was a man who later became a good friend, Bert Schultz. I showed him the bone and asked him what kind of dinosaur it came from.

Since the gravels were Pleistocene, maybe 30,000 or 100,000 years old—like most Nebraska gravels—this wasn't a dinosaur bone, only a prehistoric bison bone. That, however, was enough to bring forth images of Indians, bows and arrows, war parties, tipis, and stampedes, so the bone has served me well. It sits at this very moment on the sill of my study window two feet from my eyes.

Lifelong Love

To some degree, I've never grown up. I still love to lurk around the refuse piles at gravel pits. For a while I had a wonderful character of a friend, Bojack Lubash, who piloted the dredge at a nearby pit. I met him regularly at the local tavern to see what sort of treasures his great suction tubes had pulled up from the icy waters under his dredge; petrified wood and turtles, agates and camel teeth, mastodon molars and bison vertebrae—occasionally even a bison skull. But then Bojack died, unfortunately just about the time I moved out here, when I would have enjoyed his company most.

Then, however, I found that in a way I was going to be having Bojack's treasures delivered to my door wholesale: when we built our home, one of the first things we needed to do was have our driveway graveled. Which meant that many tons of Pleistocene gravel and rock were delivered and dumped right at our doorstep.

To this day when I walk to our mailbox or out to the shop, I walk with my eyes to the ground—or rather, to the gravel. I still find the teeth, agates, rock-wood, mammoth ivory, and bones. Best of all, I always keep a reserve pile of rock and gravel to spread when a hole or rut develops, which means I have a pile of treasures I can dig through at my leisure.

My favorite part of the story we did on local gravel pits was that I could see even before it was edited that we had a hit: Izzy and Dan returned from our shoot with the floor of the rented van littered with bone fragments, bits of petrified wood, and, well, just pretty rocks. My CBS friends were hooked too.

It was a natural follow-up, I suppose that we then made a trip to the Nebraska State Museum, the very place where I had taken my bison bone when I was a boy. There we talked with Mike Vorhies, a bubbling scientist who, like me, is still a boy at heart. We wondered over the gigantic elephant skeletons—the largest in the world, all from Nebraska, where there are still hundreds of elephant remains per square mile. The fact of the matter is, as it turns out, if you live in Nebraska, there is a chance of about one in five or six that your house sits over the remains of a prehistoric mammoth or mastodon. Amazing, isn't it? It's a wonder I never tire of, and one I was delighted to pass along to "Sunday Morning" viewers.

Edifices

Other examples of artifacts from my own past were the Postcards we did on buildings. I thought about offering up a list at this point of our architecture pieces, but it's hard to figure out which ones they are. Sure, the stories about grain elevators, the Nebraska State Capitol, the baled-hay buildings of Arthur, Nebraska, and barns (especially round barns!) were clearly about architecture. In fact, those particular stories were pretty much the same story.

At one time or another I had studied all of those as a researcher in traditional architecture, so they were stories I had written long ago, but never put on television. As a boy I wandered the halls of the state's magnificent capitol and knew it like the back of my hand. Our tour for "Sunday Morning" took us places I'd never been, but the idea was very familiar.

Most vivid in my memory of that day was the horrible smell on the very highest balcony of the building's soaring tower, the consequence of the leavings of a peregrine falcon that had made its home there. And the second experience in the capitol was even less comforting.

One of the reasons I left graduate school at Indiana University in 1965 is because the graduate library building has glass floors. The building was, probably still is, a huge brick square of rooms and offices; the center court area is the stacks where the books are. Heavy steel beams carry the shelving, from the ground up (probably from bedrock up)—a lot of weight needing a lot of support. On the other hand, the floors that sort of float between and around the steel framing and shelves is only carrying the weight of a few human beings and so it doesn't need a lot of structural strength. So, they made it out of frosted glass. Glass is not a material meant to be used for floors.

I am a brave man, a grown man, an educated man. I know that I am safe walking out on an engineered floor, frosted glass or not. In fact, the panes of heavy glass are probably stronger than plywood, when it comes right down to it. But every time I stepped out onto that glass floor, my stomach did curlicues and somersaults, and I almost had to crawl from the books back to the security of the brick part of the building. I know, I know, I know: it's stupid. Why did I get such a kick out of the fragile fury of flying in an F-16 and then get queasy about walking on a glass floor? I don't know. But believe me, I do.

So here we were, my crew and I and the capitol historian exploring nooks and crannies in the building, and we go high into the tower, many floors above its gorgeous mosaic floors, and along one of the catwalks we came to—you guessed it—glass flooring. I got over that part of the walk, and then I got back over it coming down, but my stomach was so twisted by the time we got back to the ground, the day was over for me.

When we did the story on grain elevators, we didn't, mercifully, go up in one. I have admired the stark and functional beauty of grain elevators on the Plains, vertical punctuation marks on an unwritten line, for a long time. In fact, when I started the series of Postcards from Nebraska, I found that I had a note in my "Charles Kuralt On the Road" file to suggest that he do a story on grain elevators. I guess I stole the story back from him!

My admiration for grain elevators is not simply their remarkably functional, wonderfully stark architecture, but also their comforting symbolism. To me, grain elevators are temples; monuments to plenty, cathedrals of God's bounty, worship sites for Ops and Ceres. I never see and admire those verticalities on the horizontal Plains without whispering a prayer of gratitude for the generosity of The Powers that bestow such gifts on us.

Baled-Hay Construction

Twenty years earlier I published scholarly articles about the curiosity of baled-hay construction on the treeless, brickless, stoneless western Plains, so it was natural that when I found myself in Arthur County with a CBS crew, we did a story on baled-hay buildings. Such construction was popular in the Nebraska Sandhills during the early years of the twentieth century, the years of the Kinkaid Act, the last wave of homesteading on the Plains. Remarkably, the buildings are not as fragile as you might think. Many of them, built 75 years ago, are still up and in use.

The shooting of our story went well, with a couple notable vignettes. First, the most memorable scene from the piece for viewers, I suspect, was the long walk I made down the main street of Arthur, Nebraska, a center of this kind of architecture, speaking to the camera a good 100 yards farther down the street. The scene utterly captured the wonderful openness of the Sandhills, because viewers could look past me toward the emptiness of the hills beyond the end of Main Street, and because I made that long walk without a single vehicle moving in the background. What viewers didn't get to see is that I made that walk 10 times to get it right—and there were still no moving vehicles. Arthur, Nebraska, is simply not a place where you worry about a lot of traffic on Main Street.

The second memorable scene from that day in Arthur arose from the bit of tape we shot with me coming out of a church in Arthur, built 75 years ago of baled straw and still serving a congregation. As I came out the last time, Bud began ribbing me about picking up one of the commemorative coffee mugs for sale in the entry hall of the church for $5.

"Buy a mug, Rog," Bud prodded. "You owe these people a little something. Put $5 in the pot and get a mug. It's the least you can do."

I finally caved in, put money into the pot, and took a mug. As we got back in the car, Bud complimented me on doing the right thing. Joking, I said, "I took a mug . . . but I didn't put any money in the pot." Everyone laughed.

Then we went to lunch in the local dining room, a very nice place for such a small, remote town, I might add, and as we sat down, the sheriff drove up and entered the room. Our camera on that particular series of Postcards was not Izzy Bleckman but Ray Brbiesca, a remarkably talented eye behind a camera, a man with some real adventure stories of his work in civil rights coverage—all the more chilling because Ray's Native American heritage is clearly visible.

Ray tells, for example, of the time he was covering a Ku Klux Klan rally and was confronted by The Grand High Kablutznik of the gathering, who asked, "What kind of nigra are you, anyway?" Another throwback in a sheet peered at him by the light of the burning cross and said, "He looks like one of them Hawaiian nigras to me." Ray said he affirmed that that was indeed the case, discretion on that occasion surely being the better part of valor, that he was indeed one of them Hawaiian nigras!

The Sandhills is not always a good place to be an Indian. Ray must have sensed that. Or more to the point, I think Bud made a dramatic point of the notion that Ray was in hostile country. So, when the sheriff came into the café and I wondered why he was approaching our table, Ray muttered into his salad, "I know what's he's thinking. He's thinking, 'Someone stole a coffee mug from the baled-hay church, and my bet is it's the big Indian!'"

Actually, the sheriff had heard we were in town and was just there to offer us a pleasant welcome, and to eat.

The story about baled-hay construction evoked a lot of mail; about as much as any other five Postcards put together. Everyone wanted me to write and send them the details on how one builds a baled-hay building. Unfortunately, my research had been done and published long enough ago that I couldn't conveniently dig it all out and make copies for my viewers, but I did try to send along some references. Most of all, I told them that I wished them luck, because if I were in a position of building a small, wonderfully efficient building as a cabin or home again, I certainly would consider the advantages of baled hay!

Architecture Archetypes

Same with round barns. I had studied them in great detail in the 1960s, so it only seemed natural to tell Postcards from Nebraska viewers about the fascinating things I learned about these unusual structures. There are many advantages to round buildings; more interior space for the same amount of material put into the walls, less wind resistance (and out here on the Plains that is an important consideration!), easier access and egress, and great open interiors that are for all the world like the soaring openness of Europe's Gothic cathedrals.

Less obvious as architecture pieces, perhaps, are the stories we did on ghost towns and abandoned school buildings across the Plains. Actually, therefore, on buildings that often aren't there any more! Or won't be for long.

One of the last Postcards from Nebraska was a sad one for me, about our old town hall in Dannebrog, built in 1929. It wasn't particularly distinguished architecturally and it was getting pretty battered, but it was one of the few brick buildings left in town and was a landmark. Visitors always had their photographs taken in front of the old cannon in front of town hall.

One of the agonies of living outside of town (not paying town taxes and therefore not entitled to vote, or maybe even complain) is that I have to suffer the constant idiocies of the village board in silence. So it was with pain and regret, but no recourse, that I watched the shortsighted in town insist on razing the fine old building to put up—good grief!—a tin building in its place.

Somewhere in the struggle to save the old town hall or erect a new one, everyone lost sight of what was happening. It became perfectly clear that the new building would cost far, far more than repairing the old one. A wealthy local made the fantastic offer to buy the old town hall, restore it, make it available for community use, and donate land for a new town hall elsewhere. But by that time the battle had become one of egos rather than good sense. The old town hall is gone; the new architectural atrocity is up.

There was a time, I noted in my Postcard, that towns and villages demonstrated their pride in their civic buildings, like the old Dannebrog town hall, built when money was tight and times were hard. "Let this building be a symbol of our hope and confidence in our community," the builders seemed to say.

Dannebrog's new tin building says pitifully, "Look how much money we saved!"

We also did stories on examples of architecture that aren't really buildings. Tipis, for instance. Is a tipi really architecture? I did a story on a tipi maker, noting that, like the round barn, these are tents that offer uncluttered space, strength against adverse weather, and efficient use of materials in an area where materials have always been at such a premium. I got to make yet another cathedral metaphor, too: I know the tipi in my own life as the worship space of the Native American Church, as splendid and dignified a cathedral as I have ever visited.

How about fence posts and windmills? For those of us who are serious students of folk architecture they are. All man-made structures are, not just houses, churches, or business buildings. And frankly, there are many of us who consider such structures far more splendid aesthetically and functionally than the fancy junk modern architects rear (and I use that word on purpose) to their own glory. How about a brick sculptor whose work is a part of buildings? Did a story on one of those!

The House Mover

We even sent a Postcard on my own house. The land I bought near Dannebrog in 1974 didn't have a building on it. I moved in a nineteenth century log house, smokehouse, and outhouse, and built a couple sheds over the years, but when time came to move here, we needed a house house.

Being who I am, an inveterate salvager, we looked around the Dannebrog area for an abandoned farmhouse. We found one about three miles north of town for the grand sum of $350. It came complete with stained glass and etched glass windows, so we considered it a good deal. We ran into some minor problems moving it, but the whole process was worth getting to meet the house mover, Butch Williams of Hastings, Nebraska, a genuine character if there ever was one. Now, is a guy who moves architecture around the countryside like chess pieces a matter of architecture? In Butch's case, I think his story was more a matter of the human condition than one of wood, brick, and mortar.

For one thing, I admire the notion of someone who alters the landscape around him not by simply putting up something new or taking down something old, but by shuffling buildings around as if they were hotels on a Monopoly board. And that's Butch Williams. His is a science of hundreds of tons and fractions of an inch, but he is also a man of wit and narrative, one of the best in my experience.

I think, for example, of the first time I met him, when I asked him to come to Dannebrog and give me an estimate on moving our house. He looked things over and said, "$4500."

"Should we sign a contract or do you want a deposit on the job?" I asked on that occasion.

"What good's paper if your word's no good," he said with undeniable, rural logic. And Butch was good to his word, and I was good to mine.

Another memorable moment was when Butch met Linda, who is 17 years younger than I am. "You remind me of the old farmer who married the young hired girl," he said past the ever-present stub of a cigar in his mouth. "If you ever need any loving, he told her, just step outside and fire the shotgun and I'll come running in from the field." Butch paused for dramatic effect and peered intently at the cigar butt between his fingers. "The old guy died three weeks into pheasant season."

Surprises

Bud's

I once did an entire Postcard on the cast of characters typical to any small town. Dannebrog has a pioneer heritage, a distinct ethnic orientation, a clear agricultural foundation, and a wonderful cast of characters. It is charming, it is interesting, but it is not unique. In fact, it is typical. And so are all its institutions, characters, and stories. That's what I love about it, its typicality. I am, after all, trained as a folklorist, and that's what we study—the typical.

Which is not to say there are no surprises. I wrote a Postcard from Nebraska that was no more than a rundown of our little town's characters, and it turned out to be one of the biggest surprises I had during the decade of writing, shooting, and sending Postcards from Nebraska.

The notion was simple enough and pretty much what I've been telling you so far in these pages: a small town in America is a treasure house of interesting characters, and in most towns the characters are pretty much the same. I talked about Don, Dan, Harriett, Dee, Eric, Mel . . . all my friends.

And I mentioned one of the less pleasant features of small-town life: the town grouch. At that time, in our town, that distasteful person was a thoroughly nasty, mean-spirited, angry little lout named Charlie Fox. I would've been content never to have anything whatsoever to do with him, up to and including exchanging glances as we passed on the highway or streets in town, but Charlie wouldn't let things rest that easy. He was constantly harassing my family and me. He would go a considerable way out of his way to be unpleasant to us. It didn't matter to him that none of us had ever done anything to him, or that Linda is a woman, or that Antonia was only a child. His particular brand of evil was undifferentiated.

Not that we were alone as targets of Charlie's ugly spirit: just about everyone in town at one time or another had to deal with him, so it was not simply a matter of individual discomfort or personality. Charlie was, in fact, a town institution. He was indeed the town's official grouch.

So, at one point in my Postcard about small-town characters, I jerked my thumb in the direction of his house, down Main Street and across the creek bridge, as I ran through a quick inventory of our village's cast of actors, ". . . the town handyman, the town philosopher, the town grouch . . ."

Imagine my surprise then when the piece aired and as I ran down the list on camera, found that Bud had edited in the images of the people as I mentioned them: ". . . the town handyman" (and on the screen appeared Don Hochstetler) . . . "the town philosopher" (and up came Eric's photo) . . ."and the town grouch" and there was . . . there was *my* picture!

The lesson there was that while the essayist may write a script one way, the final message and impact depend finally on what happens between the editor and producer in the editing room after the piece is shot. It took me a long time to live that one down!

I watched my step a lot more closely, doing what I could to avoid falling into a similar trap again, but when I finally did, I didn't even notice it when I saw it happen on the screen, let alone while we were shooting it. It was one of the few times in my life that I was caught totally off-guard, never saw it coming, and didn't even see it at the moment in socked me between the eyes. And again it was Bud Lamoreaux who dropped the anvil.

Full-Service Gas Station

Our story was about the small-town service station with old-fashioned service. At that time, Mel Grim was still running the station, but had it up for sale. Now, you have to remember that it took us almost a full day to shoot one of these stories, so the hours of bits and pieces that were eventually edited into five or six minutes of my Postcard were not shot in any particular order. One line might be spoken in the morning, a response later that afternoon. And I had a lot of things on my mind, including memorizing whatever stand-up lines I needed to deliver into the camera. All of which I call to your attention to excuse my innocence in this affair.

One of the things I wanted to point out in my story was that there still are places like Mel's, where he cleans your windshield when you buy gas, checks your oil, shares news of what he sees from the advantage of his station, smack in the middle of town. So for this piece I drove into the station a dozen times, got gas, asked for service, made appointments for service, talked with Mel about business, and town, and all that.

And I asked him how he felt about folks here in town who buy their gas at the discount, no-service outlets in Grand Island, a half hour away, still expecting Mel to be there when they needed help with a stalled vehicle, had an empty tank on a Sunday afternoon, or needed credit when payday was still a week away. It was a good shoot, a good conversation, a meaningful piece about small towns and small-town merchants.

Bud called me the morning the piece aired and asked me how I liked it. "Fine," I responded.

"Get the joke?" he asked.

Joke? There was a joke?

"Watch it again," he laughed, and I did. After Bud's editing and moving bits of tape around, the way my conversation with Mel went was that I talked with him about ungrateful wretches who take advantage of his generous, old-fashioned service and then buy the bulk of their gasoline in a discount station down the road in Grand Island or Kearney. Then, on our television screen, I saw myself driving up into Mel's station.

"Gas?" Mel asked.

"Just top it off, check the oil, and get the windows, okay?" I asked, which Mel did in this condensed form of our day's conversation, then watched me drive out of the station and down the street . . . toward Grand Island.

Bud thought it was hilarious.

When it comes right down to it, my recollection is that more Postcards turned out as surprises than went as expected. With as many variables as were a part of every day's shoot, as idiosyncratic and creative as Bud, Izzy, Dan (or earlier Larry), and I are, the biggest surprise over the year was no surprise. In fact, the surprises were the best part, transforming the hard work into exercises in good fun.

Dickering at the Salvage Yard

Sometimes we didn't catch the surprises until well after the event. When we did a story on Jim Stromp, the interesting character who runs the tractor salvage yard where I pick up parts for my own machines, Jim was apparently more nervous about his debut on national television than we knew at the time. I went through his salvage yard just as I usually do, finding the parts I needed, taking them off the wrecked machines, throwing them into my pickup truck, and then dealing with Jim on a price.

There is no specific, inherent value on a 50-year-old Schebler carburetor with no float assembly for a 1948 Allis Chalmers WD, for example, so there is always, inevitably some dickering that goes on.

There is a pleasant formula to it all. I tell Jim what I'm looking for, he laments that those parts are really hard to find, I counter that there are plenty of tractors sitting out there with those parts still on them so they can't be in too much demand. Stromp suggests I buy what I need somewhere else. I explain that I would but don't want to drive around forever looking for a six-dollar part. He laughs that he'll buy all of them I can find for $6, that he'll need $20—and he won't even penalize me for the stolen parts under the truck seat, on and on.

So, I found some wheels I needed, threw them into the back of the truck, and went to Jim's little office building to get the bad news about what I owed him. He came out, looked over the parts, did a quick calculation, announced the figure, we bargained a little, I paid up, and we drove out of Jim's yard with our treasures. Pretty straightforward.

It was only afterward when we looked over our footage that we realized that a very nervous Jim Stromp looked into the back of my truck, saying, "Well, that wheel over there is really hard to find, and I'll need $30 for it. These two are $20 each. That one you can have for $15. That's a total of . . . let's see . . . thirty, two at twenty, a fifteen . . . that's . . . uh . . . carry your one . . . $55 . . ." We bargained a little, not having much time, and finally settled at something like $45. Having started $30 low to begin with!

I later mentioned to Jim that he had made something of a miscalculation when he shot me the original price. In keeping with his general spirit and system, he said it was okay . . . that he would just cheat me out of an extra $30 somewhere down the line. What a guy.

The USS Nebraska

Another nasty surprise that came to me by way of Bud, an editor (often my favorite, Al Bolisky), popped up (literally!) in one of the two essays I managed to pry out of CBS News outside the state of Nebraska. (The first was the Wounded Knee story just across the state line in South Dakota.) A trip to New Bedford, Connecticut, for the commissioning of the magnificent (and terrifying) new Trident class nuclear submarine, The USS Nebraska.

The visit to the Nebraska was one of those marvelous opportunities that constitute the real rewards of doing something like Postcards from Nebraska; being able to tour that huge, powerful ship under the leadership of its commander was an experience of a lifetime for me.

For the Postcard we interviewed some of the crew members from Nebraska and showed as much as we could of the interior; as you can imagine, much of the ship is highly restricted and our tapes were previewed after the shoot by a Naval security officer. All in all it was a good story, and one of the most dramatic moments was when the captain showed me how to handle the periscope.

I turned it, raised it, and pressed my eyes to the eyesight—and Bud cut from that moment to a shot of a bunch of cows in a Nebraska pasture, as if I were taking the submarine up the Middle Loup River and drawing a sight on an enemy dairy herd! I don't suppose most viewers even noticed. But I did.

Off-Camera

The best Postcards from Nebraska surprises happened off-camera, however. You can't put together four guys who like each other and know each other well, time and time again, without having something notable, if not funny happen now and then!

For example, I am a Nebraska, rural driver. I once went to a school for racecar drivers, but generally I'm a moderate driver. Izzy, our usual driver, is from Chicago on the other hand, and he drives hard. So hard, in fact, that he picked up a few speeding tickets over the year. So many, in fact, that he was at the ragged edge of losing his license if there were one more transgression.

On receiving one of his tickets, just a few miles down the highway from my farm, Izzy tried to impress the state trooper when handing over his driver's license by saying, "I'm with CBS News. Work with Roger Welsch on his Postcards from Nebraska? In fact, we're on our way to Roger's place right now."

Utterly deadpan, the officer handed Iz back his license—speeding ticket attached, saying, "Say 'hi' to Rog for me."

At any rate, we were making a long, hard drive all the way across the state of Nebraska, 450 miles from Omaha on the Missouri River to Harrison, the most northwestern town in the state, on beautiful Highway 2. We were headed to Harrison to Sioux Sundries to do a story on what claimed to be the largest hamburger in the nation, their 28-ounce monster; seven quarter-pounders in one bun. "Eat two," they told us, "and we'll give you the third one free!"

Bud was driving because Izzy was nervous about the fragile status of his license. We were moving right along: Highway 2 is always virtually deserted, is an excellent road, and, what's most important, Bud is from New York.

We flew past a little old lady with blue hair, driving a huge, yellow gunboat of an automobile, and approached the crest of a hill just in time for . . . eeeek! A highway patrolman! Bud broke out in a cold sweat as he saw out of the corner of his rearview mirror, just as we dropped over the brow of the hill, that the patrol car was whipping a quick U-turn behind us.

"We were doing a good 85 miles an hour," Bud said quietly—30 miles an hour over the speed limit. We settled down to await the inevitable and well-deserved wages of sin. The trooper came over the hill again behind us, and pulled behind the little old lady in the huge yellow car. He turned on his flashing lights, and he stopped the little old lady!

As you can imagine, we gave Bud a terrible time about his unchivalrous behavior: "Wouldn't a real gentleman have stopped and gone back to explain the situation and rescue the poor old lady in distress, after all?!" Well, no, he wouldn't, and he didn't.

And then while we were shooting our story at the food counter of Sioux Sundries an hour or so later, in came the teary-eyed old lady, bewildered about why she'd gotten a speeding ticket when she had been so careful about observing the speed limit and driving so carefully. It was, she wept, wringing her hanky, the first ticket she'd received in a half-century of driving and . . .

Well, Bud hasn't been allowed to forget his scurrilous behavior since.

Some Ugliness

It may have been on the same trip that another part of the traditions of our little Postcards from Nebraska unit developed, one that would have been funnier if it hadn't been so chilling at the same time. As I think about it, it was funny within our group because we know we love each other—really do love each other as dear friends. But in view of what the event represented, it made us all the more determined to protect each other from those less loving in the outside world.

We had just finished a story on a miniscule wide spot in the road that had once been a booming city of some size. Its economic base, mining of natural resources, had vanished 70 years before and now little remained but a skeleton of a ghost town, almost all of which belonged to the man I was interviewing, who had up to that moment been a thoroughly pleasant, interesting fellow.

"Isn't it incredible that this town that once had 5000 citizens now has less than five?" I marveled.

"Yes," he mused. "Life is full of incredible things. For example, isn't it incredible that the people who killed Jesus are still walking the face of the earth?"

Holy moley. I've lived in Nebraska all my life and am pretty well inured to bigotry, racism, religious narrow-mindedness, intolerance, and the other ugly things that characterize ignorance. But it had been a while since I had heard anti-Semitism put quite that bluntly. In front of a Jew, a colleague, a friend.

I suspect the statement was not one of cruelty, with the knowledge of Izzy's religion and heritage; people who hold and express such stupid opinions more often than not have never had anything to do with a person of the persuasion, stripe, or witness they are attacking. In short, this idiot had probably never met a Jew in his life. He probably would have been astonished to learn that this talented, thoroughly pleasant, balding little guy with the camera was precisely one of those people "who had killed Jesus," in the medieval nonsense he was echoing 1000 years later.

I suppose we gentiles should have risen in indignant fury at the slur, but frankly, we were all so stunned by its abruptness, its idiocy, that we were utterly flummoxed. All of us, usually so glib and open, were struck silent.

As I recall, there was a cold discomfort moments later when Izzy, Larry, Bud, and I got back into the van, the hateful, implied threat still ringing in our ears, our own silence still embarrassing us. "Well," said Iz, finally breaking the silence, "if it'll do any good, and if I haven't done it before, I apologize to you guys for killing Jesus."

"Buy me a beer and I'll consider everything square," I laughed, and that was pretty much it.

Still, while we laugh to this day about how stupid the man's insult was, behind our laughter is the haunting reality that, like it or not, we're closer than we might know to those who, given the chance, would throw away any promise of brotherhood and gleefully embrace the hatred and prejudice of the holocaust.

Some Goodness

On the other hand, another Postcard carried with it some surprises that reassured me—all of us, crew, staff, and viewers, I suspect—about the fundamental goodness of mankind. Over the space of a couple years I had seen stories in our local newspapers about a mysterious trucker labeled "Heavy Duty," who had made long-distance friends with some senior citizens in a nursing home by sending them postcards from various points along his travels around America. The stories increased in number and length and finally in appeal, as the residents of the nursing home in Schuyler, Nebraska began to try to learn the real name of their trucking friend.

Every week or so, the anonymous long-haul trucker sent them a postal card from somewhere. Not much by way of a message, just a simple greeting; a little information about his load, travels, or destination perhaps, and something about the town pictured on the postcard. On a couple occasions he whipped his pen pal friends into a frenzy by noting that he had driven by their home a week or so before and waved to some of them sunning on the front porch!

The postcards were saved and put on a bulletin board in the home. Groups organized and worked to learn more about Heavy Duty's travels and the towns he visited; the oldsters combed his postcards for clues. They figured out that Heavy Duty was a Nebraskan, that he had a wife and at least two children (who occasionally traveled with him), but little more.

I could see that this was a wonderful story—but an impossible one. There was no way I would ever be able to find out the identity of this man; could we do a story about someone we couldn't find? Bud decided we could, and we did.

We talked to the people in the nursing home and listened as they told us about their appreciation for this unknown friend, how they too sought to find out who he was. They made a big sign on a piece of plywood and put it out by the highway in front of their building, begging Heavy Duty to stop by and make himself known, so they could tell him in person how grateful they were for his attentions. We interviewed truckers and stopped at truck stops, looking for our elusive philanthrope.

It was a nice story, as it turned out. We talked on camera with some other truckers (no Heavy Duty, of course) and sent out our thanks as best we could, not having any idea if he would ever see our story or hear of our search for him.

As it turned out, there were a lot of surprises ahead for all of us. First, I received letters from other nursing homes—a couple dozen, in fact—reporting that they too were friends of Heavy Duty, that he sent them postcards every week or two as well. Busy guy, this Heavy Duty!

And I got notes from people hinting that they might know who Heavy Duty was. I did what I could to follow up leads. Most of them wound up in dead ends, some simply petered out without response. And then, out of the blue, I got a response from Heavy Duty.

He wrote me a postcard, saying that he had indeed heard about the show, that he wished to remain anonymous, that (wisely, in my opinion) he did not want to reveal himself to his elderly friends for fear of destroying the mysterious fun of his good deed. That he sent cards regularly (or perhaps more accurately, irregularly) to three dozen nursing homes all around the eastern half of the nation, that he appreciated my attention, had been to Dannebrog . . . and perhaps, should he come again, he would look me up. Maybe.

I don't recall how long it was before I heard from Heavy Duty again, but it was a good year or two. Dannebrog was in the middle of its Grundlovs Fest, its annual celebration of Danish Independence Day, and the town was full of visitors. I had just finished signing books at the Little Mermaid Gift Shop and had stopped at Eric's Tavern for a beer with a tableful of tourists. I looked up to see an unlikely person approaching me, a very attractive young girl, not the sort of person one normally sees in a tavern, or even in a little town like Dannebrog.

I thought that perhaps she wanted me to sign an autograph, because she came directly toward me and stopped at my chair. She leaned over and whispered in my ear, "I am Amanda, Heavy Duty's daughter. He's drinking a cup of coffee and eating a cookie over at Schroeder's bakery. If you have time, he'd like to meet you."

It was one of the few times I can recall when I abandoned a full, cold beer on a summer day! I ran behind the girl as she went out Eric's door and went two doors down to Schroeder's. And there I met Heavy Duty.

Wonderfully, he turned out to be just as nice a guy in person as his good deeds suggested he would be. He was—is—gracious, modest, kind, and generous. He became my friend. In fact, I became a kind of conduit for him. As you can imagine, the number of people who wanted some way to speak back to their benefactor has only increased over time. But Heavy Duty couldn't give out his address without giving away his identity. So we made a deal: if he would give people my address and give me his, I would pass along mail to him, and I have been doing that now for five years since we first sent the Postcard.

Heavy Duty is still out there out the road, hauling freight, sending his cheering postcards to nursing homes. I hear from him now and then—got a card from him yesterday, in fact. And all around the country there are still seniors who await his postcards and messages.

As it turns out, Heavy Duty has an agenda. He once went to a nursing home to visit someone and was stopped on his way out by an old man who told him that his sons would be coming to visit him any moment now. The old gent rambled on and on until an attendant finally led him away and rescued Heavy Duty from further narrative, and explained that the old man had no one. No one was going to visit him because no one ever visited him. His children ignored him in his dotage just as they had all his life.

Heavy Duty stewed on that story a long time and then decided that he had to do something for the thousands of other elderly people like the abandoned old man in Kearney, and that's what he's doing.

The real lesson of that Postcard, it seems to me, is how little it takes, how small the gesture, to correct an enormous wrong, to make the world a substantially better place. A bunch of postcards, a buck's worth of postage stamps, a couple lines about a very ordinary life, a little time, a little effort. Anonymously, with little thanks and some trouble and effort, Heavy Duty is out there somewhere on the highways, doing what he can to brighten the lives of a lot of people.

Especially mine.

Worth Another Visit

We did one of our very few follow-up stories on Heavy Duty; with so many stories begging to be reported, it was hard to justify doing two pieces on one idea. But Heavy Duty was worth a follow-up. Thing is, we almost had more of a story than we wanted.

We found Heavy Duty's rural home on a bitterly cold, very windy day. We had some coffee and rolls with the family, interviewed Heavy Duty and then went off to get some footage of him driving his rig. He was between runs, so his trailer was empty and we could all five (Heavy Duty, Iz, Dan, Bud, and I) jam into his roomy cab.

Everything was fine as we drove east on Nebraska's Interstate 80, a ferocious westerly tail wind pushing us along and not giving us too much noise for our interviews and conversation with Heavy Duty.

But, when we'd finished the work and needed to go back to his home, we turned north on an access road. And the gale-force wind hit us on the side of the truck. With its empty trailer. We traveled cautiously and slowly, but suddenly with remarkable calm we later noticed, Heavy Duty, said, "She's going . . . Hang on . . . We're about to go over . . . Our left wheels are off the pavement. Here we go . . . We're going over . . ."

He said it so placidly that we hardly realized the situation we were in. As he tried to slow the rig, we encountered a state highway department vehicle, which promptly slowed and did a U-turn. They explained to us later that when they saw us coming down the highway with our left side lifted completely off the ground—several feet off the ground—they decided they better come back and pull any survivors out of the wreckage!

Once we all were apprised of how close we'd come to slamming onto our sides on the pavement in that truck, our conversation for the rest of the day was quiet, and our prayers that night were mostly expressions of gratitude!

Nebraska's

There were Postcard from Nebraska surprises that carried with them a certain amount of humor, even if it was a kind of ironic, nasty humor. There were also some perfectly glorious, heartwarming surprises. I still remember the day we did a story somewhere in the neighborhood of the very small, north-central town of Halsey, Nebraska.

We needed to head south the next day for another story in Callaway, and a quick look at the map suggested we'd have to go a good deal out of our way to get there. We stopped, however, at a tiny filling station in Dunning. The mechanic there pointed a couple hundred yards down Highway 2 and suggested that we take the unnumbered county road (paved all the way) to Arnold. "Save you a lot of miles," he said, "and it's a nice road."

"Nice" road is scarcely the word. It turned into my favorite road in this entire state. It was great enough that along the way we encountered a husband and wife team on horseback moving a herd to new pasture, interviewed them, and got great shots. But then, not far north of Arnold, we found ourselves in the middle of some of the most glorious scenery I had ever seen in this state, which is notorious for its boring vistas. Or perhaps more precisely, its non-vistas. In fact, we eventually did a story simply on this piece of road and its beauties.

Another bit of surprise beauty fell in our laps while we were doing a story on the Oregon Trail. We had shot one scene near the trail's beginning in Nebraska City on the Missouri River, and now we were 400 miles west, in Morrill Pass at the foot of Scotts Bluff, within sight of the Wyoming border. We had just shot one of my on-camera speeches a couple times, hurrying to beat a storm that was sweeping in from the Plains east of us. We finished just as a heavy rain began to pound down, and we ran full tilt for the cars. I was behind the crew because they were shooting toward me; they near the cars and me across a steep, narrow canyon.

As I began my scramble, however, I looked to the east and

realized that if we turned the camera around and shot to the east instead of the west, we could capture me standing there on the Oregon Trail, right in the middle of one of its most important milestones, with a beautiful, full 180-degree rainbow arcing right behind me!

I screamed over the wind, rain, and thunder for the crew to come back out, and once they made out my words and looked to the east, they came running. The rain was letting up as fast as it had come on, and now we had to scramble to set up the shot before the rainbow disappeared. We screamed instructions at each other in frustration. We snarled and argued. The camera rolled. I smiled. I delivered my lines perfectly. The sun came out, the rainbow disappeared, and . . . we had the shot! Sometimes things like that do work out!

Victories and Veterans

But not always on camera. Probably the biggest snafu of all the setup work I did over the years getting ready for our four-day expeditions was one I did for the anniversary of V-E Day. I remembered when I was just a child, being in the main intersection of Lincoln, Nebraska, when the news of Victory in Europe arrived. Traffic stopped. People danced in the streets. There were songs and tears, cheering and snake dances.

I lined up a reporter from the Lincoln paper who remembered the occasion well and was on the scene reporting the event. Everything was glorious. Bud suggested that we also go to the newspaper and get shots of some of the celebration on Lincoln's main street. "Surely there must be plenty of them," he said, and we were all sure there must be.

There weren't. As it turned out, there was no celebration on V-E Day in Lincoln. Everything was quiet. I must have been thinking of V-J Day. Hmmm. Well, Bud saved the day by deciding that what we would use all our footage for a piece on Memorial Day instead, and that worked out wonderfully. We wound up with a very nice story, ending up in the Dannebrog cemetery at the grave of a young Dannebrog man who died in a plane wreck shortly before the war ended.

An unpleasant little surprise, but with a positive ending, right? Well, that's not the end of the story. The real climax of the piece happened well away from the cameras and viewers. A couple days after the piece aired on Memorial Day weekend, I got a letter from a woman in Minneapolis, Minnesota. She told me in soft but powerful words that she had been watching the show as she always does, when she was astonished to see on the screen the gravestone of her young husband. He had left her widowed when he went down in his warplane, so tragically short before the war had ended. Happily married again, she said the story still brought back to her for a moment the triumph and terror of those days when what seemed like the entire world was at war. And her letter brought back to me what I could only sense in a visceral way when I was the little boy on the main street of Lincoln on, uh, V-J Day.

The Violin Maker

Perhaps the prettiest, most pleasant surprise came as we were shooting our Postcard about master violin maker David Wiebe, of David City, Nebraska. There was never any question but that we had a good, easy story going for us. David was a marvelous interview—articulate, comfortable, confident. The context of his shop was equally telegenic. The sounds of David working at his wood made the piece almost perfect. But then came the pièce de résistance—someone to play the cello he had finished just that morning. What's more, Shauna Rolston is not just a master musician, but a beautiful woman; just the thing to put the icing on the story.

But I had not yet discovered the real wonder and beauty of what we were about to witness, the first playing of a virgin instrument. For some reason it had never occurred to me that every master-instrument has its first playing. I suppose because it's not something that happens very often, especially with witnesses, never with a video camera present. Stradivariuses, Amatis, they have all had their first playing, and here we were, about to hear the first playing of this Wiebe cello.

We set up in the elegant parlor of David Wiebe's stunning Victorian home and we heard music. Not just music, but elegant music, beautiful music, from a beautiful instrument giving forth its first voice, in the arms of a beautiful woman. Wow. Even now, many years later, it gives me goose bumps just to remember it!

Mine

By and large, we were remarkably lucky during our 10 years of producing Postcards from Nebraska when it came to weather and health. Sure, we faced cold and heat, wind and rain, clouds when we needed sun, sun from the east when we needed sun from the west, but I can't recall a single situation where we were stopped dead in our tracks. A tribute, in large part, to the hardiness of Dan and Larry Gianneschi, sound technicians, Isadore Bleckman, cinematographer, and Bud Lamoreaux, agitator.

On a couple of occasions we went into a week of shooting with me just recovering from a cold, or headed toward one. Once we shot a set of pieces with my foot in a cast after I broke it by dropping a huge hunk of firewood on it, but in general, this old body held up pretty well during our shoots too.

Except twice.

We were in Grand Island after a day of shooting, running across South Locust Street toward the El Tapitio restaurant when I stumbled a bit and, I thought, twisted my foot. But that night the pain continued to increase until I was in agony. All I could imagine was that I'd broken my foot yet once again. The next day we were in Grand Island shooting some stand-ups and I was in such pain I called Linda to buy and bring me a pair of crutches and some pain pills, which she did.

What's worse, that afternoon we shot a piece on converting Nebraska's corn into ethanol alcohol, a promising gasoline sub-stitute. Which meant that I had to climb up and down the stairs of the huge distillation plant a couple dozen times, every step an exercise in horrible pain. It was a long, long afternoon.

There's not much of a climax or moral to the story: it was gout, an infirmity I have suffered from for decades and yet which I fail to recognize 90% of the time. I have no idea why, but I inevitably think it is something else creeping up on me—sprains, rheumatism, old age, whatever—and then when it finally dawns on me, "My God, it's that damned demon again," I'm writhing in agony.

Whatever you remember about how funny it was when the Captain from the comic strip The Katzenjammer Kids got gout, no matter how little sympathy you have because gout only happens to rich people who eat and drink too much, forget all that. It isn't funny, and it's beer, sausage, and beans that bring on the horrible pain, so there. (Also, did you know that "Katzenjammer" translated literally from German means "Cat howlings" but really means "hangover?")

But that wasn't the worst bout we had with bad health while working on Postcards from Nebraska. Not by a long shot. Although, curiously, the worst experience I had was only a discomfort at the time, not even close to the magnitude of pain I had with that gout episode. How serious was it? Well, serious enough that I can remember the exact date it happened, April 15, 1996. I hinted at the event earlier, in these pages, and now here's the rest of that story.

We had just shot a story on the Center for Rural Affairs in Walthill, Nebraska. It was a brisk, windy day, but warm enough so you could sense the arrival of spring. The story was a little difficult in that we had to slog around in the mud of a farmyard and deal with prying conversation out of a reticent, shy farm boy. But it was our first of four shooting days (a Monday), and the next day's story was one I'd been looking forward to for a long time. It would give me a chance to spend some time with my old friend Louis LaRose, manager of the Winnebago Tribe's bison herd.

Following the day of shooting with the farmers, we headed toward South Sioux City, Nebraska, where we had reservations at just about my favorite hotel in Nebraska, the Marina Inn, directly overlooking the beautiful Missouri River. We checked in. I had a large comfortable room with a splendid view of the mighty Missouri River only a few yards away, and we met for a good supper—rare steaks and good, red wine. We laughed and laughed, talked, and laughed some more. Louis surprised us by showing up for supper, and with his wonderful, Native American wit, made us laugh yet more, certainly setting the scene for an easy shoot the next day. After our meal, we went to our rooms to get a good night's sleep for the next day, which promised to be fairly easy. The weather forecasts were good and the hotel was only a few minutes from where we'd meet Louis in the morning, a few miles away on the Winnebago Reservation.

I woke up about midnight feeling very queasy. Not exactly nauseated, not even really sick, just uncomfortable. There was an oppressiveness in my stomach—too much food, too much wine, too much laughter, I supposed—a tightness in my chest, a blurriness. I got up and went to the bathroom to get a drink of water and regain my bearings. It didn't help. In fact, I began to feel worse. I got up again, and felt even worse.

Yes, you know what was going on, and I suppose I did too, but like just about every other human being on this earth, I wasn't prepared to think about The Truth because I wasn't anywhere close to being ready to die. Certainly not now, when it would be so inconvenient!

I thought about calling Bud for help, but I didn't have his room number and I didn't want to bother him if this was just a matter of my own overindulgence, which I still presumed it was. I worried that if I called Izzy he would shift into his Jewish mother mode and insist that we call an ambulance to haul me to a hospital somewhere, thus destroying everyone's sleep and disrupting the next day's shoot that I'd already spent so much time setting up. I thought about calling Dan. I did have his room number because we had gone there the evening before to look at footage we'd shot. But I just couldn't face the silliness of calling attention to my own overindulgence if that's all it was, or to the fuss if the reality was . . . well, you know.

The Show Goes On

I got through the night and was ready to go the next morning, when my friends loaded up their car. I felt pretty battered, still a little shaky, the light seemed peculiar, and my chest was still oppressed, but I was going to be okay. And I did make it through the day, telling Bud a couple times that I felt a little queasy. But again the day was so beautiful, the bison so magnificent, Louis so articulate and wise—no sense in making a fuss.

We shot another story Wednesday and a fourth on Thursday. I continued to feel uneasy. As we shot my on-camera speeches in a blazing hot brickyard, I had trouble maintaining my focus, misdelivering my lines again and again. I am usually pretty good at learning lines and delivering them, but not this day. I was glad when the week was over and Iz, Dan, and Bud left so I could get some rest and pull myself together.

Linda was concerned about my continuing discomfort, and now I was too. This had been going on too long. I didn't improve over the weekend, and when Linda insisted we go to see a doctor first thing Monday morning, I was ready. In fact, if there was reason for Linda to be angry with me, it was because I was too ready.

We went to Grand Island as soon as Antonia left for school, and the doctor saw me at once. He listened to my heart and looked at me in a way that I understood. "Go directly to this cardiologist's office," he said. "The doctor will meet you there." He said this in such a calm way that while we were both concerned, Linda didn't know yet what was up.

Dr. Kirrubakaran is usually not in his office until late morning or early afternoon, but Bill Lawton must have told him that he needed to see me soon, because he was there shortly. He took one listen to my chest and told me to get over to the hospital's cardiac ward at once and check in. No more self-delusion. Linda asked what she should be bringing me from home if I had to stay overnight. She was scared, as was I, but always alert to necessary details. That was when she had reason to be upset with me: "You don't have to bring anything," I admitted. "I have my bags packed in the trunk of the car."

I had known all along I that wasn't going home that night, that I was one sick cookie, and that I'd done something hopelessly stupid in putting this moment off. But now I was ready to deal with the reality. I was having a cardiac "incident."

There's no reason to go on about this because it has little to do with Postcards from Nebraska. I had a bout of "atrial flutter," the top chambers of my heart having gone into a desperate shudder instead of beating as strongly as they had for the previous 60 years. Because of my idiotic delay, a clot had formed in the top chambers, which took six months to dissolve. I was in the hospital a short time, but the main thing was that I was going to have to make some major changes in my lifestyle; less tension, more exercise, less food and drink.

At that point I took on a new load of common sense and lost a load of weight—over 60 pounds. I went on a new exercise program, cut back on stress-producing work, reestablished weakened contacts with the spiritual guidance of my Omaha Tribal friends and relatives, and reordered my priorities and concerns.

On one hand, if I had died during my interview with Louis LaRose, it would have been a sweet, poetic irony, since I hope to be buried in a blanket on his buffalo range and return to Nebraska's sweet grass as soon as possible to feel the thunder of the great beasts above me. On the other, well, I still have some things to say, so it'll be nice to be around a little longer, too!

ADDRESS

MP

Rejected
Scripts

New York / Nebraska

Over the period of my Postcards, 10 years at this writing, only three pieces have been shot but never aired. Curiously, one of those was also one of the first four we shot, with Kuralt producing. It was one of my favorites. And it established an unfortunate tenor for all Postcards from Nebraska to follow.

My field is humor. Most of my writing is humor, but very few of my Postcards have been humorous. I attribute that to my disappointment when my piece about inviting New York to be Dannebrog's sister city went down the toilet.

The script was about Dannebrog asking New York City to be its sister city. Our intention was to organize a World's Fair, the idea being that New York has the name and we have the parking. But our village's invitation got no response from then-Mayor Koch. We figured it was just more of that infamous New York rudeness.

However, a reporter for an Omaha newspaper decided to write up the story and called Mayor Koch's office to find out what had happened at that end. The man who answered the phone at Koch's office was not amused by our proposal, noting that New York City considers itself more sisterly with places like Tokyo or Paris than Dannebrog. Well, great—we just got out of a war with Japan and have never been out of war with France, if you listen to the French, but New York considers itself kin with them rather than us good ol' American farm boys.

So, in my Postcard script, I noted that this sort of snobbery has its consequences. A relationship, friendly or unfriendly, works two ways. For example, Lyle and Dora Jean Fries were planning to go to New York that summer for vacation, but because of the rudeness of Koch's office, they decided not to. "And," I noted in my script, "Lyle and Dora Jean are big eaters. So when New York figures up its tourism figures at the end of the year and comes up two people short, that was Lyle and Dora Jean. And, Mayor Koch, you have no one to blame but yourself."

I thought it was funny. The folks at CBS—in New York City,

one might note, didn't think so. And the piece never aired. As I say, that constituted a change in what I thought I would be doing. Humor was virtually eliminated as a possibility. Any time I wrote a script that was meant to be funny, Bud explained to me that we don't do humor, that humor is Bill Geist's realm, and that I stick to essays. This was an enormous disappointment to me, and an enormous mistake for our series and for "Sunday Morning." The truth is, as anyone who understands humor, culture, science, or life knows, it is people without humor who cannot, and should not, be taken seriously.

Mistakes

I'm thinking here of big mistakes, not little ones. In 12 years there were plenty of little ones. And plenty of blame to go around. And plenty of people watching "Sunday Morning," more than eager to show how smart they are and how stupid we are. I mispronounced the words "chimera" and "consummate," for example, and the letters poured in.

On the other hand, when linguistic purists wrote in to complain that the name of my town in Danish is "dan-uh-BRO," not "dan-uh-BROG," Charles Kuralt noted that I probably have a pretty good idea of how to pronounce the name of my own town, the one where the main street is named Roger Welsch Avenue. And, he further noted, names like Paris, Berlin, Prague, and Gothenburg have taken on their own distinctive pronunciation in their American manifestations. (I was grateful for his protective spirit.)

I got insulting letters from rabid vegetarians every time I was seen eating meat, and nut-case Americans every time they thought they spotted me driving an import car. I tried to respond politely that while I respect the rights of other people (including one daughter) to not eat meat, it is scarcely any of their business that I do.

Same with my hair. How, in a land of freedom like America, does someone come to the point where they think they have any right whatsoever to tell someone else how to wear their hair?! And, I wrote to the pissers and moaners, we have four vehicles in our garage and farmyard: all American-built Fords.

Bud made a few mistakes of his own. Like the sounds of a meadowlark over the picture of a robin, for example. The worst one—and the one I heard the most about—was a reversed bit of tape in our story about jerky makers. Thus, an image of my summer kitchen in use clearly showed the unlikely physics of the chimney on the woodstove sucking smoke down *into* it, rather than puffing it out.

Some Postcard stories shot but not aired were not as

complicated. We thought we would make a regular habit out of shooting a conversation at the big table in Harriett's Cafe, just the locals sitting around discussing what's going on in the world. We thought it would be a nice perspective from the small town, rural point of view. Well, we found that the folks who are effusive, witty, opinionated, and articulate on a daily basis around that same table do not do all that well in front of a camera. I suppose I could have used that line of Kuralt's: "Just forget there are five million households on the other side of the camera." But it turned out that wasn't even the worst of our problems.

By the time we got the tape back to New York and Bud had supervised the editing and we got the Postcard onto the schedule, and the Sunday came for it to air . . . our timely issues were no longer of interest. In fact, they were no longer remembered. Some Postcards have gathered dust on CBS shelves a full year before airing. Things just happen too fast in today's America. Today's CBS. Dumb idea.

There were a couple more scripts along the same line. Dumb ideas that never made it. Can't be upset about that.

A little less understandable—sometimes a lot less understandable—are the scripts that were never shot, let alone broadcast. Now and then the problem was mine. I write for the printed page, and I can tell you for a fact that writing for the printed page is not writing for television. I know writing for the page; Producer Bud Lamoreaux knows writing for television. In the case of my "Sunday Morning" Postcards, I write for television, so most of the time I desperately needed Bud's guidance.

But there have been a few occasions when, I feel to this day, my scripts would have made good television but Bud did not. Experience is a valuable, even invaluable, asset in something as complex as television essays. Unless it becomes a barrier to new ideas, in which case no wall is higher. That was sometimes the case with essays I wanted to do, but which never were shot.

First, an example of one of my mistakes. I wanted to do a story about parking in Dannebrog. We don't have parking meters, or parking lots, or parking limits. Here, you just park. Usually right in front of wherever you're going. Huge loads of hay park on Main Street. I was once moving a windmill and stopped at the tavern, taking up maybe 15 parking spaces for a few hours. No one said anything.

In Dannebrog we park on the wrong side of the street. We park parallel where the lanes are marked diagonally, and park diagonal where they're parallel. We stop in the middle of Main Street to talk with pedestrians or people in other vehicles, sometimes turning off our engines because we intend to sit and chat a while. No one makes a fuss about that sort of thing in a small town.

I think that would be a great story. Many people have suggested the same idea, also thinking it would make a great Postcard. Bud didn't think it was a good idea, and we never shot it.

This time he explained the problem to me, and he was absolutely right. I will try to pass along Bud's thesis to you, but in decidedly more diplomatic language. Small-town parking is curious and would probably be of considerable interest and amusement to people in the cities. And I have seen all of these crazy things myself, so I know they happen.

The problem is, all the various permutations of wacky parking don't happen on any particular day, certainly not the day CBS is in town to shoot a story. Parking anomalies happen one at a time, a parallel-parked windmill last month, a hay truck next month, a load of hogs in a stock trailer the day before yesterday: hours, days, weeks, years apart. There is no way a CBS News crew, here for five days to shoot four stories, could possibly find enough parking adventures to make a Postcard. We could probably shoot a parking aberration every time we see one, and tuck it away on a special reel to eventually glue all together for a story a couple years down the line, but . . .

The Cottonwood

The one essay I will always resent not shooting may still find its way to tape. The moment Bud can't make a trip to Nebraska to shoot a series, whenever I can feel confident he won't be able to be in his office to resist editing the raw footage or cancel scheduling an airing for the piece, then I will get my chance to shoot my Postcard on the humble but beloved cottonwood tree.

I'm partial to trees anyway. They are alive, you know. Most people forget that. They tend to lump trees in with rocks and houses and rivers as inanimate objects. (To be perfectly honest with you, I disagree with that too, but that's another matter. My point in this essay would be that trees are living compatriots of ours.) Maybe it's because I have spent most of my life on the Plains where trees are still relatively rare.

I shouldn't even say "still" because there are far fewer treed areas in Nebraska now than there were during earliest settlement. For millennia, annual grass fires burned away young trees, maintaining a climax grass prairie. Whatever stray saplings the fire didn't get, feisty bull buffaloes, eager to test their necks and horns against something, anything that could offer a little resistance, rubbed, battered, tore, and broke them to tattered shreds.

Primrose Farm, my farm, is a certified tree farm. We grow mostly fuel trees—ash, hackberry, locust, maple—trees I suspect I will never in my life harvest. That's okay with me. My love is planting trees and watching them grow. I love my fireplace but I can't imagine cutting down a living tree to feed it.

I did a couple Postcards about my fireplace and shot several scenes on its hearth. In one story I commented, for example, how on special occasions I haul in a piece of wood cut from an ancient, crumbling log cabin I once dismantled and add it to the fire. As I stare into the flames, I think of what that tree saw when it was alive in the very early 1800s, how buffalo may have rubbed against it, or perhaps an Omaha Indian used it as shelter while he watched Lewis and Clark pass through his territory.

I imagine the tree being cut down shortly after the Civil War by a homesteader, and what the wood then witnessed as a part of the homesteader's log house. I bask in the heat the fire is releasing from energy stored on warm days 150 years ago.

So, while I have all kinds of feelings for all kinds of woods, my heart belongs to the lowly cottonwood. Its soft, grainy wood has little commercial value other than for making loading pallets. Most cotton-wood trees are too twisted and short-trunked to be useful for lumber. Besides, cottonwood lumber has a nasty reputation for warping.

Pioneers, who had little choice in where they found their lumber, complained that a cottonwood plank left lying on the ground would warp as the bottom was moistened by the earth, and flop over. Then the sun would dry the wet side and the dry side would get wet, and it would flop over again. In a short time, they said, a cottonwood plank would thus flop its way off over the horizon, merely finding its way down the road.

To solve the problem, some settlers trained dogs to herd cotton-wood lumber, much as other dogs were trained to work sheep or cattle. Others, more inventive, cut their lumber in the woodlots or along the creeks and rivers, and stacked it with a keen eye so the wood would warp and flop its way directly to whatever building site they intended!

I once bought a couple loads of firewood—"white oak"—from some buddies. Well, I wasn't so naive that I couldn't tell this wasn't oak, but I couldn't figure out precisely what it was. Hackberry maybe? Sycamore? There are a lot of sycamores around here. But the wood burned quite nicely. It left a bit more than the usual amount of ash, but it was clean to handle, and clean burning. The price was low enough that I wasn't about to complain, but my curiosity finally drove me to ask: "What the heck is this wood anyway?" And after some friendly jostling, they admitted—it was cottonwood.

I shouldn't have been surprised. Cottonwood is our most common tree on the Central Plains; in fact, it's the Nebraska state tree. Indians appreciated cottonwood for lodge and tipi fires because it doesn't pop and throw sparks, a very important factor when you're sleeping in a buffalo robe a few feet from the fire.

Perhaps that explains why the cottonwood was sacred to so many Plains tribes. The central pole of the Plains Sundance is cottonwood. A Lakota friend told me the cottonwood leaf is a design for both the moccasin and tipi, sent to the Indian from God. Indian children chewed the July "cotton" of the cottonwood like chewing gum.

These days Plains dwellers are not so charmed by that cotton (although Willa Cather called it "summer snow"). It clogs porch screens and air conditioners and radiators. And since each of the tiny parachutes carries a seed, by late summer billions of little cottonwood trees are taking their shot at survival, usually right where no one wants a cottonwood tree.

In the state capital, Lincoln, it is illegal to plant the Nebraska state tree for that very reason. Isn't that a hell of a note? Illegal to plant the state tree in the state's capital city.

Well, not quite. You can plant male trees. They don't throw "summer snow." But by law, in Lincoln, Nebraska, the gentle and gregarious cottonwood is doomed to lead a bachelor life.

For my proposed Postcard from Nebraska about cottonwood trees, I wanted to show "a year in the life" of the cottonwood. Its long winter sleep when it is covered with ice and rattles like wind chimes, its early spring leafing, when heavy but unspectacular flowers burden its limbs, its remarkable summer growth, the July cotton. The yellowing for autumn that begins already in early August, the carpet of baby cottonwoods on the Loup River's sandbars, the squirrels' nests and wood duck homes the trees provide, the warmth of its wood in the winter fireplace, the cool of its shade in summer . . .

Okay, maybe it's a little sappy (you should excuse the expression) but the cottonwood is my arboreal hero and I would have liked to honor it with a "Sunday Morning" Postcard. Look out, Bud Lamoreaux. Miss just one shooting session, take one month off sometime . . . and you'll find yourself watching a Postcard from Nebraska about the lowly cottonwood. And I bet it'll win an Emmy.

An Afterword
and Lament

Each and every year I sent my Postcards from Nebraska to America, I also wrote a letter to Charles Kuralt. Actually, I wrote many letters to him—he was a friend, after all, to whom I owe a lot. He was also a friend of the family, so I kept him up on what was going on with Linda and Antonia, in Dannebrog and across Nebraska, and he told me what was going on in his life, doing what he could to make it seem less remarkable than mine. He was that kind of guy.

But somewhere during the year every year I also told him yet once again that I was grateful for what he had given me. And every year I told him that if it should all end, for whatever reason, I would never feel anything but that gratitude. What other faculty members at the University of Nebraska, habitués at Eric's Big Table Tavern, or columnists for *Successful Farming* magazine have had a chance to appear regularly on national television, on a prestigious television series, to express opinions, experiences, and concerns almost without restraint? I knew Kuralt had given me a Life Gift. I felt that way after the first year of Postcards from Nebraska; I feel that way, even more so, now, after ten.

And I am sad about what has happened to Charles Kuralt's dream show. And to the idea of Postcards. Charles's original notion was to bring to America those things he loves (jazz, books, humor, drama, art, good reporting, good books) as seen through the eyes of his friends—Billy Taylor, John Leonard, Bill Geist, Eugenia Zuckerman, the CBS professional journalists. His thought was that there are people even in little towns tucked away in the middle of nowhere (like Dannebrog, Nebraska) who need and enjoy solid culture and sound information delivered, not by pretty faces, but by real people.

At the bottom of it all, he gave Americans credit for good sense and good taste and the ability to use their own minds to sort it out. All those things happening at the centers of culture and sophistication—the grand cities of the world—would not be lost on those who happened not to be living in those centers, he figured. I think he was right.

Somewhere along the line he decided that there are also things happening in the villages and on the rural countrysides that might be of interest and importance too to the people of the cities, and that's where I came in. He called my pieces "celebrations of the ordinary," and as a folklorist interested all my life in the power of the typical, the substance of the traditional, I had no trouble at all with that idea. My goal and purpose on "Sunday Morning" was to show people things happening in my clearly unremarkable little town of Dannebrog in the most ordinary of states, Nebraska, that would make them think, maybe even say, "Wow! Who would expect something that interesting (or beautiful or important) to be going on in that little town of Whatever, in that state . . . what is it? Kansas? Or Iowa? Whatever."

I never discouraged that kind of confusion. Bud always insisted that I mention Dannebrog and Nebraska somewhere in my scripts but to my mind, what mattered was that our viewers know that the extraordinary is actually very ordinary, that the ordinary is actually very extraordinary. To me, my Postcards were never about Dannebrog or about Nebraska. They were about the power of life in small towns everywhere.

Appreciation of the Ordinary

Somewhere along the line all that theory and idealism was lost, along with the luster of "Sunday Morning," its ratings, the power and integrity Kuralt brought to the show, the good minds and plain faces. And the fatuous, shallow minds of the people who eventually came to run "Sunday Morning" were never more obvious than the degree to which they misunderstood what Postcards from Nebraska were about.

It's not surprising. They probably could have faked an understanding of conventional high-culture snobbery, but an appreciation of the ordinary was forever beyond them. So, the original message, "See? There are important things going on in your little town and in your state too. Look for beauty and wisdom where they are unlikely. You'll find them there too," was lost. Postcards from Maine appeared, thus saying, I guess, "See? There is also beauty where it is obvious and kicks you in the face." Some message. Some story.

And then as if even that were too subtle, there were Postcards from New Orleans and Colorado. Never mind that you'd have to be a complete idiot not to find interesting cultural events, items, food, and scenery in places like that.

Eventually I came to feel, however, that this incredible stupidity was not stupidity at all. I now feel that these dull lumps of people, devoid of imagination, romance, or curiosity, aren't simply too dumb to understand the nature of Kuralt's idea about the power of the common community and its common citizenry, but rather too arrogant to accept the idea. They saw the thesis and rejected it, which is even more stupid than not seeing it. I can only hope that all television producers of this weary sort will spend the rest of eternity in the company of Martha Stewart, making Christmas bouquets out of old milk cartons reassembled with a glue gun for their Cape Cod style houses' doors. Thing is, they'd probably be perfectly content with that level of intellectual challenge.

Bitter? Yeah. "Sunday Morning," Postcards from Nebraska, and Charles Kuralt were such beautiful, unique, important contributions, and they were replaced by such empty silliness. I can't imagine anything but bitterness. It's not easy to complain, whine, and pule about something so grand as those halcyon days of "Sunday Morning." But neither is it easy to let them be destroyed without complaint.

And that's not to say that there is also not still that gratitude. I am grateful for those years when I watched "Sunday Morning" with delight that commercial television, otherwise such a wasteland, could still offer a home for such an oasis. I am grateful to have been a part of it. I am grateful to whatever powers in this world, or outside this world, that let me call Charles Kuralt a friend and "Sunday Morning" a friend. Maybe there'll be someone else another time like Charles Kuralt who'll have the foresight, power, and patience to put together another show like "Sunday Morning."

Never another "Sunday Morning," never another Charles Kuralt. There'll never be anything like them again. But something like them. And maybe there'll be something like Postcards from Nebraska too.

Appendix

I haven't kept very good accounting of these dates, and apparently neither has CBS, since some of these are clearly not precise. Some of the listed dates don't even fall on Sundays! I obtained a list from CBS but it omitted several items I had on my list, so there are almost certainly stories I have forgotten that they have misplaced too. But this will give you some idea when the various stories aired.

No.	*Postcard Titles*	*Dates*
1988		
1.	Postcard sample	February 18
2.	Overalls	May 8
3.	Bullet holes in road signs	May 22
4.	Big table	June 12
5.	Coal trains	July 24
6.	New humor	August 21
7.	Rain	September 10
8.	Small-town characters	October 23
9.	Pickup trucks	November 12
10.	Naming children	December 11
1989		
11.	Fireplace	January 8
12.	Country auctions	February 12
13.	Abandoned schools	March 5
14.	Sandhills cranes	April 10
15.	Plains youth	no date available
16.	State poet	May 5
17.	Windmills	June 9
18.	Parades	July 2
19.	Bluegrass lawns	July 30
20.	Dannebrog Country Club	August 8
21.	Wildflowers	September 3
22.	Pawnee bones	September 16
23.	Mari Sandoz	October 10
24.	Nebraska football	November 5
25.	Ghost town	December 3
26.	Farm dogs	December 10
27.	End of the year	December 31
1990		
28.	Big burgers	February 4
29.	Antique shop	March 25

	30.	Airports	April 13
	31.	Potter	April 22
	32.	House mover	June 3
	33.	Tornado alley	July 15
	34.	Fishing	July 22
	35.	Kitchens	July 29
	36.	Sandhills	August 12
	37.	Produce stands	no date available
	38.	Milkweed	no date available
	39.	Omaha powwow	no date available
	40.	Small-town newspaper	no date available
	41.	Harvest	September 23
	42.	First gentleman	October 28
	43.	Engine #3985	December 6
	44.	School Christmas pageant	December 20
1991	45.	Winter in Nebraska	January 20
	46.	Country veterinarian	February 1
	47.	Kaleidoscope artist	no date available
	48.	Gulf War in Dannebrog	January 29
	49.	School bus	March 3
	50.	Spring	March 17
	51.	Arbor Day	April 18
	52.	Garbage	no date available
	53.	Fancy chickens	May 24
	54.	Return of Gulf War vets	June 11
	55.	School reunions	no date available
	56.	Canoeing Nebraska rivers	June 26
	57.	Grain elevators	July 21
	58.	County fair	August 21
	59.	Fence posts	September 22
	60.	Greek festival	October 6
	61.	Horseshoe pitching	no date available
	62.	Lou Sabin	October 20
	63.	German POW	November 10
	64.	Oregon Trail	December 1
	65.	Heavy Duty	December 15
	66.	Christmas lights	December 22
1992	67.	Smokehouse	January 12
	68.	Village board	January 26
	69.	Omaha handgame	March 1
	70.	Economic boom and bust	March 15
	71.	Barns	March 29
	72.	Late snowstorm	April 26
	73.	Harriett's Cafe	May 24
	74.	Election	June 7
	75.	Windmill factory	June 21
	76.	State capitol	July 5
	77.	Missouri River	July 19
	78.	Detasslers	August 2
	79.	Gravel pits	August 16
	80.	Red Cloud	August 30
	81.	Antique farm show	September 20

	82.	Small-town wedding	October 4
	83.	Six-man football	November 1
	84.	County sheriff	November 15
	85.	Omaha Symphony	December 27
		and Omaha music	
	86.	Raising ostriches	no date available
1993	87.	Mel's service station	January 12
	88.	Gulf War vet home	January 30
	89.	Ethnic food	February 14
	90.	Blacksmith artist	March 7
	91.	Spring is here	March 21
	92.	Violin maker	April 11
	93.	Soup contest	May 2
	94.	Back roads	May 16
	95.	Cemetery	May 27
	96.	Salvage yard	June 13
	97.	USS Nebraska	July 15
	98.	Meteor crater	July 16
	99.	Rural addresses	no date available
	100.	Band concert	August 1
	101.	Windstorm	August 29
	102.	Nysted	October 3
	103.	Cornflake	November 7
	104.	Ponca Tribe renewal	November 21
	105.	Water witcher	December 4
1994	106.	Monks	January 2
	107.	Farm family	January 23
	108.	Bald eagles	January 30
	109.	Quilters	March 13
	110.	Longevity	April 24
	111.	Steakhouses	May 15
	112.	Circus	June 12
	113.	Mammoths	June 26
	114.	Salmon farm	July 23
	115.	Indian animators	July 24
	116.	Litter pickers	July 31
	117.	Fight for water	August 27
	118.	Stock car driver	September 4
	119.	Widow's harvest	October 23
	120.	Dannebrog redux	November 27
	121.	Working dogs	December 11
1995	122.	Player pianos	January 8
	123.	Blacks on the Plains	February 5
	124.	Baseball strike	February 19
	125.	Ted Kooser, Plains poet	March 19
	126.	Photo curator	April 2
	127.	Baton maker	May 14
	128.	V-E Day	May 28
	129.	Murder in a small town	June 4
	130.	Rooshen bottoms	July 2
	131.	Waterfalls	July 23

	132.	Indian summer camp	August 20
	133.	Highway 2	September 3
	134.	Baled-hay construction	October 15
	135.	Farmer-warrior	November 12
	136.	Squash	December 3
	137.	Grandma's birthday	December 24
	138.	Small-town movie house	December 31
1996	139.	Brand inspector	February 4
	140.	Ethanol	March 3
	141.	Cowboy boots	March 31
	142.	Wild horses	April 14
	143.	Tipi builder	April 21
	144.	Land Link	June 9
	145.	Buffalo man	July 14
	146.	Salt marsh	September 1
	147.	Vise-Grip pliers	September 15
	148.	Hal Holoun	September 29
	149.	Corn pickers	October 27
	150.	Tarzan poet	December 1
	151.	Old trains	December 15
1997	152.	Brick sculptor	March 9
	153.	Slow tractors	April 6
	154.	Honey bees	June 15
	155.	Tractor lady	July 6
	156.	John Janovy	August 17
	157.	Crazy Horse	September 21
	158.	Stone tracks	October 12
	159.	Polka King	November 1
	160.	Fruitcake	December 7
1998	161.	Brick streets	March 1
	162.	Zoo school	April 12
	163.	Knife maker	June 14
	164.	Turtle Lady	July 12
	165.	Rural mail	July 26
	166.	Lady welder	September 6
	167.	Heavy Duty revisited	December 13
1999	168.	Unicameral	January 17
	169.	Spanish Polkas	February 7
	170.	Small-town librarian	April 4
	171.	Sandhills golf	June 13
	172.	Jerky boys	August 8
	173.	Corn cobs	September 12

Dates Unknown

Rural sociology
Architectural civic pride
Neihardt center
Wright Morris
Civic mortality
F-16
Sacred Pole